EXPERIENCING TAROT

Dr Roopa Patel is a practising Tarotologist, who has written numerous columns appearing in several magazines and newspapers (including *Femina* and *The Sunday Observer*), and made several TV appearances, including Siddharth Kak's *Mano Ya Na Mano*.

She discovered Tarot quite accidentally and experienced startling insights and powerful connections with her being. Today she believes that Tarot is a powerful tool for spiritual growth and guidance.

She is married and has a nineteen-year-old son. She lives in Mumbai.

Experiencing Tarot

Roopa Patel

Artwork by The Singh Twins

Collins

An imprint of HarperCollins *Publishers*

First published in India in 2011 by Collins
An imprint of HarperCollins *Publishers* India

Building 10, Tower A, 4th Floor, DLF Cyber City, Phase II,
Gurugram Haryana – 122002, India
www.harpercollins.co.in

ISBN: 978-93-5029-175-7

2 4 6 8 10 9 7 5 3 1

Typeset in Adobe Caslon Pro 11/14
InoSoft Systems Noida

Printed and bound at
MicroPrints India, New Delhi

The book is dedicated to my parents who nurtured my spirituality from childhood and encouraged me to have an enquiring mind.

Contents

Preface

Many years ago, a young colleague at the British Council where I worked suddenly said, 'Ma'am, I think you should write a book on Tarot.' Surprised, I looked at him and said, 'Yes, if I had ten arms like Devi Durga and a hundred heads like Hydra, I would think of it!' I laughed his suggestion off as even the thought of it was inconceivable. I was stretched for time … really stretched, with an exciting but demanding job at the British Council, where I handled nine portfolios as the Head of Arts. I had a young son who needed attention, a home that had to be set up (for we had just bought a flat), a husband who had given up his job and needed support as he was starting a new business and a father who was seriously ill. To add to the demands on my time were servants who regularly disappeared and a Dalmatian (bought at my husband's whim and my son's insistence after seeing *101 Dalmatians*), who was growing up into a huge monster—I did not know what to do with him in a Mumbai flat! Somehow, despite all this, I was able to juggle writing my Tarot columns and doing Tarot consultations, but that was my limit. I thought I could not take on anything else.

Yet, my young colleague's suggestion lingered; it registered in my mind although it was forgotten at a conscious level. When I retired from the British Council, the idea suddenly came back to me. I knew what I wanted to write. I outlined my concept and then started searching for a publisher who would be interested. Friends suggested Mita Kapur, who runs Siyahi, a literary consultancy. And the rest is history. I am grateful to Mita for all her help. I am immensely grateful to HarperCollins and Sheema Mookherjee for having faith in my writing and finding it worthy of publication.

I also appreciate the encouragement of my friends who were confident that a book would emerge, however discouraged I was at times.

My son has seen many a client come home and has taken Tarot in his stride as a part of his life. My husband, on the other hand, had many misgivings about Tarot, but even he consulted the oracle when the going got tough! I would like to thank them both for accepting the intrusion in their family time with such good grace.

Finally, I must thank my students, who believe in me completely and my work with Tarot.

Talking About Tarot: An Introduction

The world that we face today is a chaotic and confusing one. Older values have collapsed and new ones are not enduring enough—we are groping in the dark, looking for something to give us respite and peace. What we need is some guidance, a solution, some help on a deeper level. It is here that Tarot touches. It is here that Tarot heals.

In the times that we live in, it is important that we heal the myriad scars that mark our psyche if we are to be happy and bring some sanity into this world. You are the world and the world is you. Unless we heal ourselves, we cannot do anything for anyone else, for we are impacting the world and the world is impacting us. All the trauma, violence, acts of terror and cruelty, and ills exist in the world because of accumulated pain that has not been addressed or healed. The pain knots into a hard ball and then explodes. It is vital that we do not allow our pain to harden and then distort and destroy us and the whole world.

What we need to learn from Tarot are techniques to help us understand the self, to know our strengths and weaknesses, who we are and what our path is. We need to learn ways of healing and ways of improving our lives. It is from this understanding that change can happen. An awareness is generated that will ease our pain—only we can turn our lives around, but we will need to take responsibility and work for this change. If we go that way, then Tarot and other esoteric sciences will alleviate the pain in human lives and help create a better world.

Section I

My Journey

Tarot just happened to me. Many years ago, knowing about my interest in unusual things, friends holidaying abroad brought me a deck of Tarot cards as a gift. In the early 1980s, Tarot was unheard of in India. Very few people knew what the cards even looked like. I had some vague, nebulous idea of what Tarot meant but nothing more, and yet I felt drawn towards the cards. I guess there was nothing really strange about that. The pictures, the symbols and the colours would fascinate anyone who saw the Tarot cards for the first time, and I was no exception. They came at a convenient time, when I had just completed my postgraduation and was thinking about my career path.

My desire to know more about the cards impelled me to write to my relatives in other parts of the world. They sent me a lot of material on Tarot, such as workbooks, interpretations, meditation exercises, philosophical meanings and esoteric resolutions of Tarot. What started as a curiosity became a passion as I read everything I could find on the subject.

What fascinated me was the idea that the cards could form a bridge between the conscious and the subconscious mind and convey messages that could guide and help one to live a better and more meaningful life. These were strange ideas and I knew I could not accept them without questioning their veracity and experiencing their truth myself.

I come from a family where we had the intellectual freedom to think and believe what we wanted to, but we had to justify our thoughts and beliefs on the altar of reason. My father, a man of intellect and an admirer of J. Krishnamurti, the great spiritual teacher, constantly challenged our thoughts and encouraged us to question every aspect of the world around us. My mother is a woman of faith. Our dinner table conversations usually centred on the topic of *bhakti marg* versus *gyan marg* or faith versus reason. Therefore, I questioned the truth of Tarot, not once but many times, but I was not fully satisfied with the answers. There was something that I could not put my finger on, and that was my fascination with Tarot. The more I probed, the more questions I had and the fascination persisted. There was something about the cards that affected me deeply. I felt connected to them—I was intrigued.

My search led me to explore various alleys, many books and exercises, until finally I felt ready to experiment with the cards in the areas of divination and guidance. I did three to four spreads (a specific layout of cards in a pattern is called a spread) for myself, asking questions pertaining to different areas of my life. But whatever question I posed to the oracle, it was answered by the same card, the card of ill health. I was perplexed, irritated and finally convinced that the cards were not in any way connecting to my questions. I put them away, thinking that I had come to the end of the journey. I was in perfect health and there was absolutely no reason for that card to appear.

You can imagine my shock when within a month, I found myself in the Intensive Care Unit of the Jaslok Hospital in Mumbai! We lived in Jabalpur, Madhya Pradesh, and I had to be brought to Mumbai under medical supervision. I was almost unconscious and seriously ill. A low-grade fever, which had been completely undetected, had developed into a major illness called miliary tuberculosis.

For over a week, I lived in the twilight zone of delirium and high fever, but then, very slowly, I recovered. The first thought that came to me when my head cleared was—how did the cards know that I was going to fall ill? What were they trying to tell me? What would have been the result had I taken the warning of the cards seriously and had got myself medically examined? Would I have avoided this suffering and ill health? All these questions raged in my mind.

The experience affected me greatly and I started looking at Tarot with new eyes. Still, I had to understand the way it worked. I had to find my own vocabulary to express its essence. I had experienced something unusual but it was essential to know more about it.

I did Tarot readings and noted down the cards that appeared. I also noted down the guidance each card offered and went back to it later to see how it had worked out. The Tarot cards came up with rare insights, startling perceptions and simple solutions to problems posed to them.

I started doing Tarot readings for friends and people who came through friends and slowly, the word about my interpretations spread. Somehow, a newspaper got wind of it and their journalist Carol Andrade, did a story on me in the *Afternoon*. Soon, I was flooded with requests for Tarot readings.

The logbook that I kept helped a lot in my research. I entered each reading that I gave seekers and requested them to give me feedback and tell me how it worked. Almost seventy to seventy-five per cent of the feedback showed that Tarot had amazing results. For instance, a retired high court judge from Dehradun, who came to Mumbai for a hernia operation, had an amazing experience with Tarot. Then there was a beautician with a startling yet beautiful story. There are several such examples which showed how uncannily Tarot worked, stories which I have narrated in the third chapter of this book.

There are also some instances when Tarot did not work. When someone tried to hide the truth, the cards that appeared were disconnected. If someone tried to trip the oracle by asking false questions, the cards did not reveal anything. I recall a woman who actually wanted to ask about her extramarital affair, but pretended that her lover was her cousin, and another woman asking about her illegitimate child, but saying the child was her husband's. The cards that came up had no pattern, no sense and no story to tell. They were random cards with no meaning. It was only when these people confessed that the cards changed dramatically.

I have discovered that Tarot works best when you approach the cards objectively, with respect and an open mind, with neither belief nor disbelief. All you need to have is a sincere desire for knowledge.

Section II

How Tarot Works

Every human being is born with a predetermined outline of their life, a broad framework called destiny, which is fixed. But within this framework, a lot of modification and change is possible. Human beings have free will—we can choose our actions. Our actions beget reactions and a chain of action–reaction propels life in a particular direction. Tarot helps us make the right choices and do the right actions. When we are at a crossroads, the wisdom of Tarot shows the way and helps us to take the reins of our destiny into our hands. It is like a hand of cards dealt to you, which is fixed and cannot be changed, but winning and losing the game depends on how you play your cards. Tarot helps you choose and play the right card at the right time and win the game of life.

The human mind is made up of the conscious and the subconscious mind. The conscious mind is the sum total of our experiences, emotions, the environment and our conditioning from the day we are born. The subconscious mind is the universal mind of the human race. It is connected to the cosmos and has complete knowledge of the past, present and future. When a human being is born, the subconscious mind is very powerful, but slowly, as a child grows up, the conscious mind with its conditioning forms a barrier, making it difficult to reach the subconscious mind. We start functioning without the power of the subconscious mind, mostly basing our actions on thought and reason, which are limited in their range. At times, we are able to make a connection with the subconscious mind and the result is creativity. All great works of art, literature, and scientific inventions and discoveries are made when the subconscious mind is activated. They have a universal appeal that is eternal because they are created from the eternal mind. All meditation and spiritual pursuits are attempts to connect with the subconscious mind. Intuition is a faculty of the subconscious mind. Instant perception is the result, which is different from a deliberate conclusion, the offshoot of thought.

Tarot works through the subconscious mind. Symbols of Tarot are symbols of the universal mind and are connected to it, helping to activate the subconscious mind. The meanings of the symbols embedded in the pictures on the cards are not arbitrary but in accord with the universal language, which is beyond verbal expressions of the conscious mind. A Tarot reader interprets this pictorial language of the subconscious mind and transforms it into verbal expression, thus facilitating the connection between the subconscious mind and the conscious mind, and conveys the messages of the subconscious to the conscious.

The twenty-two cards of the Major Arcana represent the journey that every soul takes and the important experiences of a person's life. The cards encode information that affects human behaviour—for example, The Fool embodies the archetype of the eternal child; Judgement: rebirth; Temperance: balance and healing; Strength: endurance. The Major Arcana cards deal with the spiritual aspect of life, healing, shifts in thinking, inner growth and finding solutions to problems. The fifty-six cards of the Minor Arcana look at everyday life. Most of the seventy-eight cards—twenty-two of the Major Arcana and fifty-six of the Minor Arcana—usually have an image of a living being, or some part of a human figure situated in different contexts. This figure represents not just the physical body but the mind, soul and spirit as well. The body experiences the physical world, which also impacts the psyche. Every experience leads to modification of the psyche that needs constant change and the adjustment of the consciousness to meet the challenges that we face. As this adjustment happens to every person, these experiences cross over the boundaries of an individual consciousness and expand to the level of universality. The journey through the cards' imagery is therapeutic as it adds to the self-knowledge and understanding that leads to spiritual awakening and the completion of the cycle.

Each suit of the Minor Arcana represents one of the four elements that make up the universe—water, fire, earth and air—and connects these elements through shuffling of the Tarot cards. It shows how the elements impact our lives, leading to new perspectives and understanding. The four suits of the Minor Arcana are: the suit of Wands representing the element of fire—it suggests enterprise and intuition; the suit of Cups representing the element of water—it is suggestive of emotions and imagination; the suit of Swords represents the element of air and connects to thinking and intellect; and the suit of Pentacles represents the element of earth, operating in the milieu of material reality and possessions. Each suit consists of fourteen cards: Aces, the numbers two to ten and the four court cards of the Page, Knight, Queen and King. Aces suggest new beginnings in the element of the suit that they lead—for example, water represents emotions so the Ace of cups represents a new beginning in the area of relationship or feelings; twos represent integration, harmony and partnership; threes suggest completion and unity; fours indicate stability; fives relate to the senses and testing times; sixes indicate choice; sevens are victory and achievement; eights signify endurance and strength; nines indicate material success and knowledge; and tens mean the culmination and ending of a cycle. Pages represent youth, Knights young adults, Queens indicate different women and the Kings suggest mature men. The temperament of the court people is according to the element of their suit.

In this book, I have discussed only the Major Arcana cards in some detail as they are of primary importance and connect deeply with spiritual processes.The major shifts and changes in life and thinking are reflected through the Major Arcana cards. For healing, meditation and self-development, it is these cards that are used, for they connect with the subconscious mind. A student of Tarot needs to be familiar with these cards. The Minor Arcana cards are like fillers—they complete the picture and are necessary, but in themselves are not as potent as the Major Arcana cards.

A Tarot spread is a map of your problem. The cards are shuffled, cut into three stacks and restacked from right to left and opened. They are placed according to specific positions of the spread that you have decided to use and interpreted by a Tarot reader. The most popular spread is the Celtic Cross, which is a ten-card spread. This is popular because it is a complete spread, giving full information about the past, present and future. The spread deals with an issue from different perspectives. For example, there are cards that relate how the problem started, what forces were responsible for it, how the problem is viewed by others, what you fear about the situation, what your expectations are and what the likely solution is. It reveals—through the card placement and meaning of the cards—all that you need to understand and know about the problem from all perspectives so that you can arrive at the right conclusion to resolve the issue at hand.

The guidance of Tarot comes up from the subconscious mind and intuition helps to interpret the symbols. All answers are within you and Tarot helps bring these answers to the conscious level. For this purpose, Tarot uses numerology, Kabbalah, colour association and therapy, mythology, alchemy, religious theories, ancient spiritual knowledge, medieval tantra and other psychic tools to interpret and convey certain ideas. The symbols are drawn from all these different sources and represent the journey of a soul through life. In their different combinations and permutations, the cards depict every human experience, situation, attitude, and feeling that a person encounters in life. One could use Tarot to gain esoteric wisdom. In her essay on *Tarot and Carl Jung's Archetypal Images*, Inna Semetsky says that these symbols 'act as transformers capable of raising the unconscious contents to the level of the consciousness: the meanings become explicit by the virtue of "becoming conscious and by being perceived".'

Tarot can be used for meditation, self-improvement and healing and to find a direction in life. The images on the cards register in the subconscious mind and create external circumstances to match it. For specific healing, a specific card needs to be identified and used. An experienced Tarotologist can give advice about the right selection.

Tarot Card Readings

There is great curiosity and anxiety about what happens when you go to a Tarot card reader. What should a querent (questioner) expect?

It is important to know that there are good as well as bad Tarot card readers, just as there are good doctors and bad doctors. It is necessary to check the credentials of the reader before you go to him or her so you are not disappointed or traumatized. The best way to know this is to speak to the reader directly and ask all the questions that you have. Make sure you are satisfied with the answers before you go ahead. You may also want to speak to someone who has been to the reader to clear your doubts. It is possible that despite all this care you might still choose the wrong reader, but that is a chance you should be willing to take.

If you do not know anything about a Tarot reading, you may feel discomfort, if not fear, about what you are getting into. Is it some kind of black magic? What will the reader do? Will the reader shatter whatever little peace you have by giving you dire forecasts? Will you be exploited? Will you be hurt?

To avoid these doubts, let me first put your fears at rest. A good Tarot card reading is a pleasurable experience, encouraging people to go for more readings as they feel a sense of relief. A reading can provide a deep insight into a problem and give a solution that can work. Most clients come with the feeling that their problems are insurmountable, but this despair is dispelled through the reading. A reading usually offers hope, it is not the end of the world and by some efforts a solution can be found.

Many a time, the insight offered by a reading is accurate, sometimes even startling, and makes the querent sit up and take notice. I have often noticed that the person brightens up and the body posture changes as he or she becomes more attentive, feels more safe and comforted, and begins to see some truth in what is being said.

A good reader will first discuss the problem, understand what the issue is and then proceed through the spreads to unravel it. Since there are many kinds of Tarot spreads, the reader will use the one that will work the best. The spread will tell you the root of your problem, how it started, the negative influences that affected it, what has happened with the problem in the recent past, what your fears are, the environment or context of your problem and whether it is supporting you or not, what other people think about the problem, what you want and what the outcome is. It will also tell you what can be expected in the long term.

According to the cards that come up in the spread the reader is able to cross-check with you to find out whether he or she is on the right course. You should be able to verify what the reader is telling you and it is only then that the reading will proceed. Based on all the cards in the spread, after sifting and connecting all the cards and assessing the influence of each card on the other cards, the reader comes to a conclusion that determines the best way to proceed in the matter. The conclusion is verified by a sequence of other spreads, a process that continues until all aspects are teased out and the querent gets answers to all doubts and questions. This reading becomes the beginning of a relationship and the querent keeps in touch with the reader until the issue is resolved.

I prefer to use the Celtic Cross for most of my readings though I often use different spreads, depending on what comes up in my mind. Mostly, I prefer to work with the healing aspects of Tarot by working out a Tarot profile. This helps me to discover and address whatever is laching, prescribing a card for meditation to heal the wound caused by that lack. This has worked wonders with my students and clients. I have worked with over 500 hundred students and most of them have come back with excellent results, which have been recorded.

A good Tarot reader will never tell you anything dire; rather, he or she will tell you how to find a solution to your problem. Responsible Tarot readers will never focus on any negative aspect, but will look at constructive ways of bringing positivity in your life.

Responsibility of Tarot Readers

The new age is open to receiving wisdom that the previous era was not—and this is a welcome trend. The only problem is that Tarot has become a party game. Anyone who can buy a deck and wants to gain a little popularity is out there reading cards. Tarot is a serious esoteric instrument for self-development, healing and meditation. It is a prayer to the universe and if we want it to be answered, we need to be sincere. All new age sciences are energies that have been created and discovered for the welfare of mankind. These energies will work for us only if we let them. It is the same with the environment—the trees, oceans, the earth—all the elements are there to help us and we need to have the right relationship with them. The relationship should not be tainted with exploitation. It has to be about love and empathy. The whole universe is out there to make our lives happy, but we are destroying the energies that want to help us. We have destroyed the trees and the oceans, polluted the air and the environment, corroded the natural resources and stripped the earth of all its gifts. The result can be seen in the alarming increase in the number of natural calamites and disasters. Misuse of any energy will cause a natural reaction, which can result in problems.

Divination is a calling. It is a life-long commitment. Divination will choose you, if you are required to do its work. If you are serious about Tarot it will happen, whether it takes years of work or occurs very quickly. You will be led and all you need to do is follow. Initially, it is wise to focus on healing yourself and taking care of your problems and your issues.

Once you have gained an understanding of Tarot and how it can help you, the next step would be to buy a deck of Tarot cards. Here are some suggestions to guide you towards a long, fruitful relationship with your cards.

Choosing a deck

In India, Tarot is still a recent phenomenon and only a few new age stores stock different kinds of Tarot cards. I usually recommend the Rider–Waite deck to all my students. If you want to look at other alternatives, the largest variety of Tarot card decks is available online at the website of tarotAeclectic of Australia maintained by the webmaster Solandia.

The best way to choose a deck is to let your intuition make the choice. Go with the deck that you like. Feel the cards, go through them, and see how you feel. It is a good idea to ponder over them and then, after checking out a few decks, come away without buying any and go back again the next day. Note down the deck and images that stay with you and note any dreams or feelings that come to your mind. Go by that.

There is no deck that is good or bad—you have to see which one works for you. So don't get confused. Just allow yourself to flow and you will make the right choice. It is rightly said that you don't choose the deck, rather the deck chooses you!

How to take care of your cards

When you buy a Tarot deck, you should get a wooden box to keep your cards in and a yellow or purple pure silk scarf or cloth to wrap them in. It is said that wood and silk keep away negative energy and help retain your energy in your cards, which is important because you need to build a relationship with your Tarot cards, which require your energy too.

The silk cloth should have the edges neatly sewed. You could add trimmings, if you like, to make it beautiful. The box should be aesthetically pleasing and a shape and size that you like. Remember that you are going to put in something that is very precious to you—your own self and a part of your being.

Remove the packing and purify the cards by passing them over incense smoke one by one. The best way to do this is to light three to four incense sticks at one time and slowly move the cards from one hand to another over the smoke. Reverse the cards and repeat the process. Before wrapping them in silk cloth, shuffle the cards well and allow the trapped energy to dissipate.

Look at the cards and spend fifteen to twenty minutes each day with them. It does not matter that you don't understand them yet. Just keep familiarizing yourself with the cards. There will be some cards that you like, just as there will be some that you don't like. There will be some that frighten you and some that make you feel safe. Just be aware of these feelings.

At night, remove the cards from the box and keep them under your pillow, wrapped in silk. Do this for at least eight days and write down your dreams or feelings. You may wish to start a diary and write down these thoughts as they come to you. At that time they may not make sense, but some time later you may get some startling insight from these initial inner responses. After eight days, you are ready to work with the cards.

How to begin your work with Tarot

One of the best things that you can do is to start a Tarot diary and record your daily card readings. Use a seasoned deck that has been charged with your energies for this work.

How should you bring out your daily card? Keep ten minutes aside in the morning to do this. Find a quiet corner and light an incense stick or a *diya*. Breathe in deeply about three to four times to centre yourself. Shuffle the cards well, peacefully focusing on the day, and ask the guidance of the cards about how it will unfold. Cut the cards into three stacks from right to left and make three piles; restack with the first stack on the second pile and the two on the third one. Now pick up the top card. Look at it carefully and see what it means to you. See how it connects with what you expect from the day, then look at the meaning given in any Tarot book and pick the meaning that your intuition tells you is the relevant one. Write down the name of the card with the meaning that you have picked and the date in your Tarot diary. In the evening, you can check whether the card meaning you had selected matched your day or not. At first, you may get it all wrong but slowly, you will be able to pick up the right nuances and indications that may surprise you. If you wish to work with Tarot, make this ritual a habit—it is an effective way to get to know the cards and your own connection with them. This will help you in building your intuition, and your connection with the cards.

Section III

Tarot in India

Astrology and all esoteric sciences have been revered in India for centuries. In ancient India, the practitioners of these sciences were treated as men of God and scholars who could read the stars. Even the kings would acknowledge their value and follow their guidance in all important matters. The *raj purohit* or the royal priest combined the role of an astrologer and the religious head of the kingdom. British rule saw a greater emphasis on logic and reason, which came hand-in-hand with a new spirit of doubt and scepticism. The Indian intelligentsia was greatly influenced by this rationalism and it became fashionable to look down on esoteric practices and on people who believed in this 'mumbo jumbo'. As reason became paramount, educated Indians began to distrust esoteric practices and stopped looking beyond reason for answers. Consequently, esoteric sciences found themselves pushed to in the sidelines of society.

America became the land of milk and honey, of every material comfort and luxury, the dream of every young aspiring Indian. In the 1960s and 70s, thousands of urban, educated Indians migrated to America to make their future and gain economic independence. However, with the increasing number of suicides, divorce, crime and violence, people started questioning the blind following of reason and material values and looked towards the East to gain a balance.

India today is a potpourri of beliefs, scepticism, faith, doubt, religion, magic, nationalism, logic, modernity and ancient practices, superstitions and miraculous happenings. There is a place for everything and different ideas and practices co-exist in relative peace and harmony. The country has come a long way from its traditional mindset and cannot go back to blind belief.

However, there is a need to have something that will help people understand and unravel their lives, for reason has failed to bring solutions or solace. Today's times have not provided answers to burning questions of existence. There is no resolution, no peace and no guidance. We are all searching for answers and something that will solve the puzzle of life. People have tried to find these answers beyond rationalism through Tarot, runes, astrology and other new age sciences.

Of all the esoteric sciences, astrology reigned supreme in the Indian tradition. Every event took place only with the sanction of the priests who, by looking at the ephemeris (a table showing the position of planets and other astronomical objects), worked out auspicious days based on the movement of the planets and stars. Every marriage, for instance, required horoscopes to be matched and the wedding date to be worked out. This need often led to corrupt practices and exploitation by practitioners, prompting urban, educated young Indians to question all esoteric sciences. Still, astrology continues to play an important role in the Indian way of life and even though educated people scoff at astrologers, the same people turn to astrology or predictive sciences for relief in times of stress.

Indian astrology, though brilliant, is difficult, obtuse and inaccessible to lay people as it requires years of study to learn and to interpret the planets, their aspects and signs. People needed a solution that was midway between tradition and modernity, something that was accessible and urban and yet went beyond reason in offering solutions and a vocabulary to which they could relate. In Tarot they found a perfect instrument.

Though Tarot cards were unknown until recently, India has its own tradition of circular, hand-painted, and lacquered playing cards called *ganjifa*. It is believed that the Malla kings of Bengal started this tradition in the eighth century AD, after which it spread to Jaipur, Orissa and south India. There was a revival of *chitkari* (figurative painting) and lacquer work on *ganjifa* cards in Sawantwadi, a town in Maharashtra—these *ganjifa*s are based on *dashavatara*, the ten incarnations of Lord Vishnu: Matsya, Kurma, Varaha, Narasimha, Vamana, Parshurama, Rama, Krishna, Balarama and Kalaki. A set of *dashavatara ganjifa* consists of 120 cards. There are ten suits, consisting of twelve cards each. Two are called court cards and the remaining ten are numerical cards numbered from one to ten. The set of cards is usually kept in a box decorated with pictures and motifs.

Some scholars believe that the *ganjifa* cards were brought to India by the Mughals. There is no record of their use as tools for divination, but they were used to teach people about religion. It is said that the *ganjifa* game pleased the gods. Brahmins, too, played it. There is a record of the game being played near the temple of Puri in Orissa. Various Hindu gods, characters from the epic, the Ramayana, and the nine planets are depicted in a deck of *ganjifa* cards. One theory is that gypsies took these cards out of India and used them for fortune-telling and then slowly, European, Egyptian and Middle Eastern influences changed the appearance and purpose of *ganjifa,* which over time, evolved into Tarot cards as we know them today. We have no proof of this though the theory does not seem improbable. There are some similarities between *ganjifa* and Tarot. Both have ten pip cards (Minor Arcana cards numbered 1–10). Both are supposedly related to the ten incarnations of Vishnu and have a suit related to money or coins: Pentacles in Tarot and Chandra or *Safed* in *ganjifa.*

Tarot was unknown in India until recently, except in very small pockets, in places like Mumbai and Delhi that had connections with the west. Till the 1980s, nothing much was written or heard about Tarot in public fora like newspapers or television. I still remember the time the *Afternoon* newspaper featured me and my Tarot cards on a centrespread—and I was flooded with some 100 phone calls. The first Tarot column, written by Veenu Sandal in Delhi, appeared in the 1990s in the *Asian Age* newspaper. I started the first Tarot column in Mumbai in the *Sunday Observer* at about the same time. Soon my Tarot columns appeared in the magazines *Jetwings* and *Femina* as well. For a few years, these were the only Tarot columns that existed and I did not hear of any other Tarot work in the country.

My column in *Femina* was based on a question-and-answer format and elicited letters from all over India. Satya Saran, the editor at the time, said that she would get sackfuls of letters every fortnight. Most of the letters were from educated, urban women discovering their rights and often at loggerheads with their husbands, who did not understand their independent thinking.

The *Jetwings* column was a monthly horoscope targeted towards the business traveller. The response was mellower and usually from businessmen who discreetly wanted some advice. Initially, they were a little hesitant and slightly sheepish about consulting the cards, but later they came for consultations in droves.

'Bollywood News' by Samar Khan on the Star network first started the use of Tarot on television. I was slotted a short segment after he presented the news, in which I gave the annual forecast of Bollywood stars on their birthdays. This was very well received.

The Tarot boom started in 2000 when a plethora of Tarot card readers emerged. Although they were first restricted to the mega-metros, interest in Tarot later percolated into the second- and third- tier cities, too.

The *Dainik Bhaskar* asked me to do a column for them in 2000. This column was translated into Hindi to go into seventeen to twenty-five editions all over the country, drawing a huge response from all the cities where it was read. People who came to me from these cities were ambitious and saw that Tarot as something sophisticated, new and exciting. Fed up with traditional ways, they wanted something different and more modern from life and also from the oracle they consulted. The questions they had were about their work and their progress in life, not just about marriage. They wanted to live better lives and were willing to do whatever it took for their future.

Tarot appealed to the youth in this country for it could be explained in a logical way. Also, the language of Tarot was English (I have yet to find a single Tarot book in Hindi or any regional Indian language), which appealed to the westernized generation. People were fascinated by the images on the Tarot cards, which were European in depiction, beautiful, mysterious, and appealing in their colour and style. Another reason for Tarot gaining ground is that people are more willing to try something different. Unfortunately, astrology, which has been dominant for a long time, lacked novelty. Astrologers were mostly Brahmins and represented a Hindu mindset that was not acceptable to people of all communities, though other communities also have their own ways of practising fortune-telling.

In India, Tarot is now mostly used by women, both as practitioners and clients. I have not heard of too many male Tarot card readers, though there are a few well known ones. I believe that women are more sympathetic, more accommodating and more psychic. There was a need for an instrument with an accessibility and immediacy that could offer precise information and solutions. Tarot filled this need.

Today, India has more Tarot card readers than ever before. There is a new interest in new age sciences, which is no longer a preserve of the unconventional. There is no shame attached to the esoteric, nor do people look at you askance if you say you read Tarot cards. There is a shift in the Indian mentality and people are accepting the idea that new age sciences like Tarot can provide answers which logical thought may not be able to.

The Future of Tarot in India

The most important factor is the right understanding and awareness of what Tarot and other new age instruments offer and how they work for our good and for the benefit of mankind. People need to be made aware of the real benefits that these sciences offer and how they can help alleviate suffering, pain and unhappiness in our lives. Only then will people connect with these instruments in the right way.

It is important that books are written about Tarot and other esoteric sciences. To bring about awareness of the benefits offered by these sciences, newspaper articles, chat sessions, workshops, societies, seminars, lectures, informal study groups, and discussion in the public domain can play a valuable role. Books on Tarot and other new age sciences in regional languages would have greater value. Translations of informative books on Tarot would help reach a wider audience and dispel wrong information and myths about esoteric sciences. There is a huge interest in Tarot in small towns, but there is a lack of information, resulting in misconceptions and blind followers. For instance, when I was invited to Hyderabad to talk on Tarot by a ladies' club, I realized that very few of the large crowd of women knew what Tarot was about. Most of them thought that it was something new from the western world that would tell fortunes in some way. This is a misconception that many people still have about Tarot.

Perhaps a community of dedicated Tarot readers, who can present accurate information in the public domain, is necessary to combat false beliefs regarding Tarot. When queries are invited after my talks, the main questions are whether Tarot is related to witchcraft and if most esoteric sciences are actually black magic. Such inaccurate beliefs can do great harm to the cause of new age sciences. Though an organized approach for the growth of these sciences and a formation of a body that would certify and evaluate the practitioners seems tempting, it could also lead to making Tarot and other such sciences limited, devoid of the individual freedom that is essential for inner flowering and which is the essence of these instruments. The inner mind operates in total freedom and does not fall in line with someone else's methods and systems, however good they are.

Yet I am aware that there needs to be some way of saving people from unscrupulous money-makers who use Tarot for material gain, who pretend to be genuine readers when they actually know nothing about Tarot. These concerns need careful understanding and like-minded people should come together to explore solutions.

Issuing certificates and putting a stamp on a person's spiritual maturity and ability to interpret intuitive impulses is not a happy solution. Who can certify and evaluate an esoteric practitioner? Can anyone judge and certify another practitioner? Is it possible to evaluate the inner being—from which all esoteric practices and knowledge flow—of a seeker? I don't really know ... these are questions that need to be thought about deeply.

All these esoteric sciences need research and a real understanding of how they can help the human plight. India has an august reputation in all matters esoteric. Most healing and esoteric sciences are not new at all and most of them have links with India. Right from Reiki, pranic healing, crystal healing and healing through the elements, to astrology, cards, dice, symbols, animals, trees, birds, flowers, stones—all these have been used in India for esoteric purposes. Our Vedas and Upanishads are filled with esoteric wisdom and we need to rediscover these to understand and use our heritage for the growth and development of the body, mind and the soul, suited to today's needs and mindset. Russia, Bulgaria, the UK and the USA have university courses in many esoteric sciences and parapsychology and we too, should establish such courses—but with a difference. The aim of these courses should be to impart knowledge, generating awareness of the potential of growth. It should be a take-off point we can evolve in harmony with our existence on our own terms and forge our own path in freedom by inner experimentation.

There is a need for departments at the university level to teach esoteric sciences and remove ignorance and preconceived ideas. Information about the latest global discoveries in this field should be available, discussed, explored and applied. Scholars from different parts of the world should be invited to share their experiences and knowledge. Our inspiration could be drawn from our ancient universities at Takshashila, Ujjain, Varanasi and Nalanda, all centres of learning, research, and practice. We should emulate their work and not blindly follow the west. The approach to learning should be like digging a well where the water springs from within, not a structured approach of building a swimming pool where the water is filled from without.

We need to evolve our own vocabulary and our own images for the new age sciences so that they connect with our minds. This can only happen over a period of time when various aspects get integrated. But we need to make a beginning, to water the seed that is already present in our consciousness and bring it to fruition.

Chapter One

History Myths and Legends

1.

History, Legends and Myths of Tarot

Writing about an esoteric science as vast, ancient, and controversial as Tarot is a challenge and it is really difficult to sift through all the legends and stories about its origins to find out which ones are more real and relevant. No one really knows what the truth actually is and many scholars feel that the early practitioners invented some legends as well, letting their imagination run wild! But, then, sometimes truth is stranger than fiction and I am no authority to make judgements. There are many who believe that the origins of Tarot have been quite deliberately obscured for a variety of reasons, such as the need to guard esoteric wisdom and to camouflage the real intention of the cards to protect Tarot from religious intolerance or to preserve the secrecy required to pursue certain spiritual paths.

Tracing the historical development of Tarot is easier and more precise as it is based on records and facts. For example, we know that the Tarot game was played in the Italian and French courts, with Tarot court cards adorned with images of kings, queens and nobles. The original pictures on the cards were gold-edged miniature paintings, works of great art and beauty. They were so lavish and expensive that they were often stolen—as recorded in the ledgers of the day.

It is important to remember that the aim of Tarot is to connect with the subconscious mind and this, in principle, gives the practitioner some leeway to create any image that they think will enable the connection.

The only comment I have regarding this is that if a practitioner really feels that images of footballers or animals like cats, for example, can help them connect with their subconscious mind, then why shouldn't they use them? I can only suggest that people who question this freedom should stay away from such practitioners.

Hundreds of different types of decks are available all over the world. In India, too, new age stores offering a great variety of Tarot cards have mushroomed in major metros like Mumbai and Delhi. Catalogues listing types of Tarot cards in stock are also for sale in special book stores. In my personal opinion, one of the best decks is the Rider–Waite deck because it conveys the ideas of Tarot clearly and symbolically.

The Origins of Tarot: Legends and History

Tarot has caught the imagination of mankind ever since it was created and has left an indelible impact on the human psyche for centuries. We don't even know when the oracle of Tarot came into existence. Some scholars maintain that it is just a few hundred years old while others say that the earliest records of Tarot are thousands of years old. The Tarot scholar Eden Gray says that Tarot was derived from the pages of one of the oldest books in the world, originated by Hermes Trismegistus ('thrice great'), said to have transmitted divine knowledge at the time of Moses (he is also considered a mythical figure representing Hermes, the Greek god, and Thoth, the Egyptian god) during a period when magic, astrology, and mystic sciences flourished. Greek and Egyptian traditions of magic, astrology and alchemy were combined in this book.

Popular legends about the creation of Tarot include an Egyptian one that narrates the story of how Tarot cards appeared in a dream to the High Priest of Egypt. He prayed to Thoth, the god of wisdom and magic, asking him to reveal the mysteries of the universe. Thoth answered his prayers and gave him the images of Tarot. It was after this revelation that the Egyptian priesthood adopted the study of Tarot as an intrinsic part of their course of instructions.

Another equally popular legend places the creation of Tarot cards at a conference of esoteric practitioners in the city of Fez. Held as a platform for the pagan world to unite against Christian tyranny, the conference was attended by scholars of numerology, Kabbalah, colour association and therapy, mythology, alchemy, religious theories, ancient spiritual knowledge, medieval tantra, the Masonic order as well as users of other psychic tools. They needed a secret method of communication and a symbolic language of magical practice that was hidden from the Christian world. At the time of the Crusades, Tarot became a powerful tool of the pagan world against Christian persecution. Nomadic gypsies were the custodians of this secret knowledge and carried it with them from place to place, spreading its message.

Some legends connect the Tarot to the Celtic Grail stories and believe that the four suits of the Minor Arcana of Tarot have a relevance to Christianity. The most popular legend in Wales is that of King Arthur and the Knights of the Round Table, who spent years searching for the

Holy Grail, the holiest of Christian relics. Believed to be a chalice in which Jesus Christ's blood was gathered while he was still on the Cross, the Grail had miraculous powers. Finally, it was Sir Galahad who found the Grail after many battles. The Cup suit of the Tarot cards represents the chalice, while the spear that wounded Christ has become the suit of Wands. The disc on which the cup was kept is the Pentacles and the sword of the knight who sought the Grail is the Swords suit.

The legends that are gaining popularity revolve on the premise that Tarot is Indian in origin—the word 'Tarot' is said to derive from the name of Tara, an Indian goddess, and the twenty-one cards of the Major Arcana are the twenty-one aspects of the mother goddess. The Indian god Vishnu, who is the nurturing aspect of creation, is depicted with four hands, each holding a different object—the conch shell, disc, lotus, and mace—which are said to be the precursors of the four suits of Tarot. The suits are also considered to be representations of the four castes in India.

Another very interesting idea about the origin of the Tarot is put forth by the alternative health practitioner Russell Sturgess, who suggests that Tarot cards are pictorial representations of the Sermon on the Mount from the New Testament, which a gypsy sect called the Catharis used as a sacred map of the teachings of Christ. The Catharis was later persecuted and destroyed as heretics by the Catholic Church, but left these representations as a legacy (secrecy was important so the symbolical meanings were hidden in simple images).

Tarot combines so many different ideas, symbols and philosophies, ancient learning, alchemical and magical ideas, that it is no surprise that so much speculation is rife regarding the genesis of Tarot. Even the origin of the word 'Tarot' is debatable. Some scholars maintain that it comes from the word 'rota' or rotation, the turning of the wheel without a beginning or an end—a continuous flow of time. Others believe that 'Tarot' is from the Torah, the Hebrew Bible or from the Latin word, 'to *orat*' which means 'to speak'.

Historically, the spread of Tarot began with the Renaissance when the Turks sacked Constantinople and scholars fled to Europe, armed with their books and manuscripts, new ideas and new learning. It is likely that Tarot cards were brought into Europe at that time by the gypsies. With the proliferation of new trade routes between Europe and other countries, esoteric wisdom percolated into Europe, although it was vehemently resisted by the Catholic Church. It condemned the Tarot cards as the

Devil's Picture Book and punished anyone who possessed a deck of Tarot cards. Since Tarot and other new age sciences indirectly questioned the supremacy of the Church, by showing that an individual could connect to the inner being (and soul) and seek as well as find answers without the intervention of a priest, they were perceived as a threat to the Church, which came down heavily on all esoteric practitioners. According to the Church, the priests were God's representatives on earth and it was only through their intervention that people could attain forgiveness. Tarot challenged these ideas by opening a new route for people to find themselves.

In medieval Europe, alchemy, a philosophy based on a chemical process that aimed at transforming base metal into gold, just as the base mind can be transformed into illuminated consciousness. With the focus on the powerful subconscious images of the Tarot cards, the transformation generated was so similar to alchemy that many medieval European scholars identified with Tarot and began to practise it.

Tarot Decks

The Tarot deck may have originated in 1441 in Italy as a card game called Tarocchi. It was a popular game, with different versions in different centres in Italy. Some decks were specially commissioned by wealthy patrons, who had their own images painted on the cards. These were produced by great artists, who used precious gold, making the decks substantially valuable.

The earliest historical mention of Tarot cards, according to Craig Chalquist in *The Origins of the Tarot*, is an entry dated February 1392 in the book of accounts kept by Charles Poupart, treasurer of the court of King Charles VI of France, which records a payment for three decks with gold backgrounds painted for the king by Jacquemin Gringonneur.

The earliest Tarot deck that survives today is the Visconti–Sforza deck, which was hand-painted in the mid-fifteenth century. It is believed to have been made as a gift to commemorate the marriage of Bianca Maria Visconti, daughter of Filippo Maria Visconti, the Duke of Milan, to a soldier called Francesco Sforza in 1441. There are references to both the families and their coat of arms on the deck. Historically, however, the Marseilles deck (as it was named) is considered more important since these prints carved on wood blocks have vivid illustrations of the Major Arcana.

Etteilla (Jean-Baptiste Alliette), a French fortune-teller during the rule of Napoleon, created the Etteilla deck, which is valuable because it used Egypt as a source of inspiration, promoting the idea that Tarot originated from there. His deck was created for occult purposes and not as a game. Another Tarot theorist, a contemporary of Eteilla, was a French priest called Eliohas Levi, who added Biblical and Jewish aspects to the cards. He attempted to link the twenty-two cards of the Major Arcana to the twenty-two letters of the Hebrew alphabet.

In England, the Hermetic Order of the Golden Dawn was founded in 1886 by MacGregor Mathers. Arthur E. Waite (1857–1942), the English Christian occult philosopher and a member of the Hermetic Order of the Golden Dawn, worked with the artist Pamela Coleman Smith to create a special deck featuring images, landscapes, and symbolism on all the cards. The Rider–Waite–Smith or Rider–Waite deck was very different from the stark Marseilles deck that lacked esoteric details, and is now considered the standard Tarot card deck, used worldwide.

Other decks can also be used, decks that will help you broaden your understanding of the symbolism of Tarot used by different interpreters as well as various aspects of the other occult sciences.

Early decks

1. The Wirth deck: Oswald Wirth was a Swiss occultist (1860–1943). His cards are bright and have a metallic shine. He connects the twenty-two cards of the Major Arcana to the Hebrew alphabet.
2. The Renaissance deck: Featuring the Greek gods and goddesses that form the Major Arcana, these cards are decorated with gold work that is visually very attractive.
3. The Medieval Scapini deck: Rooted in the Renaissance, this deck is a realistic representation of the first Visconti–Sforza deck. In the Renaissance style, the images on the cards are artistic, with a dream-like quality.
4. The Minchiate deck: The ninety-six (instead of seventy-eight) cards of this deck include the zodiac signs and the four elements. This gives the reader a wider scope for expanding the range of

interpretation, although it could become confusing and outside the purview of traditional Tarot.

5. The Palladini deck: Based on the art deco style of the 1920s, the images on these cards show the influence of cubism in their geometric forms, with the muted colours of moonlight that create a mood of melancholy. The significance of the cards is that they are an example of the role an important art movement of the time can play in the making of a Tarot deck.
6. The Thoth deck: Considered important for Tarotologists, this deck was created by Aleister Crowley, working with Freida Harris. It has eighty cards instead of seventy-eight, with three versions of the Magician's card. It draws consciously from other esoteric sciences like Kabbalah, astrology, the symbolism of the zodiac, alchemy and the elements. There are sexual aspects in the cards, too. It is a modern deck with symbolical colours and an unusual style reminiscent of the inner workings of the mind. *The Book of Thoth* that usually comes with it shows how to integrate with each card.
7. Paul Foster Case's BOTA deck: These cards are not laminated as the aim is to allow the reader to colour the drawings—which are only black and white outlines—according to their own inner understanding and development. Case believed that Tarot came from Morocco and was created to preserve the sacred knowledge from books that were in the burned down Alexandrian libraries.

Modern decks

1. Motherpeace Tarot: These are circular cards based on feminist ideas. They have no male images.
2. Animal Tarot: The energy of the animal world is used in this deck to interpret the human psyche.
3. Cat People's Tarot: This deck uses images of cats to divine the human mind and to activate the imagination.
4. Tarot of Baseball: The paraphernalia, figures and scenes from the game of baseball—such as bats, gloves, balls and caps or coaches, umpires and managers—is used in the suits of this deck, which treats Tarot like a game.

5. Silicon Valley Tarot: The cards in this deck include coloured caricature drawings of modern figures such as the Hacker, the Layoff, and the Nerd.

Today, there are innumerable decks available and produced every year. Each Tarot deck is a work of imagination by the creator, who aims at reaching the inner being with images that he or she believes can help the process along.

Why are there different types of decks?

Tarot is an instrument of the subconscious mind and forges connections to it for divination, self-development and healing.

Each human being has a different perspective of life and some experiences may impact them at a deeper level. Since Tarot needs to touch the core, it is relevant for each person to create their own decks, provided they know what images and associations will really connect to the core. It is possible that some of the decks created are mere gimmicks and are used to make a statement, rather than serve any esoteric purpose. If a particular deck is not what you think a Tarot deck should be, it is advisable to avoid it. Very much like art, literature, or freedom of speech, the choice is subjective, with no right or wrong. It depends on the perspective and the sincerity of the creator. If the deck strikes a chord, it will be appreciated and valued or with time, die out.

It is interesting to note that there are Tarot decks based on voodoo. There is one deck of cards that features the likeness of Martin Luther King, Jr. while another one uses the image of Princess Diana. Other Tarot card decks feature popular cartoon characters, whereas others use sinister-looking characters.

Myths and Truths about Tarot

MYTH #1: The Church banned Tarot cards because they contained secret heresies and occult magical techniques.

Any idea or practice that threatened the supremacy of religion was regarded as non-religious and blasphemous. This is true of most religions, not only Christianity. Even scientific discoveries and inventions were not accepted if they were contrary to the beliefs of a religion. The same applies to Tarot. Tarot introduced new ideas taken from many esoteric sciences, which were not accepted by the Catholic Church. It represented the new learning of the Renaissance, which was open to all knowledge.

MYTH #2: You are doomed by what the Tarot cards say.

Tarot offers guidance to improve the quality of a person's life. It helps you to understand yourself better by connecting to your issues and problems as represented by the cards. You are free to decide what you choose to do. A good Tarot reader will only give constructive advice and will not make any dire predictions.

MYTH #3: You must receive the cards as a gift.

Strange things do happen when your unconscious mind is ready to receive a gift from the universe. I did receive my first deck of Tarot cards as a gift, but I know of many experts working with Tarot who have bought their own Tarot decks.

MYTH #4: You should not read your own cards.

This myth may have some truth but not because it is considered unlucky to read your cards or any such thing. Reading for yourself is difficult because it is hard to be objective about yourself and often, the cards mirror your emotions rather than the truth. By the same token, you should not read the cards when you are in a disturbed state and unable to keep yourself balanced and neutral. As it is said in Hindu philosophy, a seer must aspire to be above *kam* (desire), *krodh* (anger), *maya* (illusion) and *moh* (attachment).

MYTH # 5: Tarot is always right.

The interpretation of Tarot depends on several factors, most of all, the objectivity of the reader. If you are the querent, your emotions often colour the interpretation and sometimes, you cannot see what should be obvious to you in a spread. At other times, the querent can decide to exert his or her free will and go against the natural flow, which ruins the reading. Tarot only predicts possibilities—what is most likely to happen.

Sometimes the cards simply will not work—perhaps God's way of telling you that you are human and can err! Sometimes, you have to take a detour to come back to the point and learn the lesson when you are ready and the cards will unfold their meaning to you at the right time. All this should be seen as a part of growing and evolving.

MYTH #6: You must have set rituals to read properly.

Rituals and ceremonies are not really compulsory. I do have a few set rituals, but that is for my own benefit, not for the cards. I have a particular way of shuffling and cutting the cards. I read the cards by going with the flow. I think the way a reader chooses to work with the cards is a personal one. It is about setting a pattern for your subconscious mind, which helps trigger the underlying emotions and feelings. Each person may feel differently about the best way to read the cards, which is fine.

MYTH #7: There is only one way to interpret the cards.

Tarot cards are just tools that help you access your intuition or the collective unconscious mind. Each card's meaning acquires a new shade from the card that goes before and after it. Also, all the cards in a spread have an impact on each other and the interpretation is the sifting and understanding of what the cards are pointing to in the conclusion. You could arrive at that conclusion in a variety of ways, whether it is analytically, intuitively, rationally, or in a dialogue with your client. Cards can be read in many ways—what matters is that you connect with your inner being and the guidance springs from there.

Myth #8: Tarot readers are witches.

Who is a witch? To my mind, a person who uses energy to harm, destroy, or damage another human being could be called a 'witch'. Every idea or action can be used for positive or negative purposes. It is the purpose and not the instrument that determines what is negative or positive. Tarot is just a tool to help you turn inwards and connect with your being to get answers to problematic questions and learn lessons about how to lead your life. There are so many other spiritual ways as well that can help you in doing this. All sciences, including the esoteric ones, can have a negative impact. Wrongly used, all energy, including that of nature, will recoil. For example, since human beings have exploited and abused nature, there has been a huge increase in natural disasters; climate change is threatening human existence; floods, tsunamis, earthquakes, drought and hurricanes have become more frequent. Every positive force has a polarity and Tarot is no different. Tarot can be used, like religion and esoteric practices such as tantra, for negative purposes by people with evil intent, but that does not mean that Tarot readers are 'witches'.

Myth #9: Tarot cards are 'evil'.

First of all, what is 'evil'? The connotations of the concept are immense, but basically it involves the intent to do harm to others—at least that is the sense as applied to the effect some people think Tarot has. On the other hand, if evil means any idea or action that does not fall in line with a set way of thinking, then all sciences, all new ideas of growth and development, all new age instruments, and everything different and new can be termed evil. It is evil for some people because it is untried and can cause discomfort and fear. However, I beg to differ—a new path may or may not be accepted by all, but does that make it evil? Think about scientific pioneers who have braved ignorance and fear, such as Galileo, who was found guilty of heresy when he maintained that the sun was at the centre of the universe, contrary to the accepted view of the time. Tarot is merely a different way of promoting inner growth and does not cause harm. Fortunately in India, I have not yet encountered such prejudice.

Myth #10: Tarot is a scam.

There are fraudulent people in all areas of life. Certainly, there are Tarot card readers who abuse the trust placed in them as do doctors, lawyers and other professionals. People are more vociferous against new age sciences as it is easy to doubt the intentions and approach of a science that is not empirical but esoteric. Unless one experiences the benefits of an esoteric science, it is difficult to trust it and I can understand this.The common argument is that a deck of plastic cards cannot be anything more than just cards, but this line of thought denies the power of symbols and the power of your own mind. Tarot cards, runes and *I Ching* are triggers for the unconscious mind to unfold and connect with the conscious mind, and are as real as radio waves or electricity both of which are also intangible. My answer to this argument is that an individual should experience Tarot before deciding whether or not to use it. If it does not work for you, reject it by all means—but trust your own response to the experience first.

Myth #11: Tarot cards are magic.

Magic could be described as the power to use supernatural forces to manipulate objects in the world, but in Tarot, it is your subconscious mind that is at work. Tarot and all other esoteric sciences are just catalysts for this magic to work by making the power of the subconscious mind available to you. Similarly, meditation is also magic—because it can transform your life.

Myth # 12: What Tarot says is infallible.

As mentioned earlier, Tarot cards do not make predictions, but only indicate the possibility of what may occur in the future. A Tarot reading is of immediate value because it operates in the living present and only gives you guidance about your future actions or what path you should take. This guidance changes with time and with your actions, according to how you have used your free will and what direction you have chosen. The best use of Tarot is when you are at a cross road and need an understanding of the situation to make an informed decision.

Myth # 13: Tarot is only for fortune-telling

This is a king-sized myth that has misled many people. Yes, of course, Tarot is also a tool for divination, but its real value lies in easing the processes of self-development, healing and meditation to enable you to know yourself better, to heal your conditioning and your circumstances with the energy of the cards and to create positive circumstances in your life through meditation. The archetypal figures and symbols of the cards help put you in touch with your fears, pain and other emotions or feelings which can be seen, experienced and then released in a safe situation.

MYTH #14: The Tarot was invented by gypsies

We have no proof that gypsies created Tarot cards. Gypsy tradition places the origin of Tarot cards in India, where they were called *ganjifa* cards and were taken out of India by these nomads to Europe. The *ganjifa* cards then got transformed into Tarot cards in Europe. This theory, however, has not been accepted by many critics.

MYTH #15: Long-term use of Tarot and other occult sciences can create a negative impact in the reader's personal life and circumstances.

Abuse of esoteric tools is bound to impact your mind and your being. If you use Tarot as a party game and treat it with disrespect and callousness, you are creating negativity in your mind, which will manifest itself in a negative way. But if you use Tarot with respect as a tool for self-development and healing, for the benefit of mankind and for the wholeness and healing of your clients, you will bring the same positivity in your life. A Tarotologist has said, 'Fear breeds fear. If the purity of intent is combined with humble action both the Tarotist and the client are protected.'

Myth #16: Nobody else should touch your cards.

Well, this is not an inviolable rule, but if you are a Tarot reader, it's preferable to be the only one to handle your own pack—as far as possible. To make it easier, you could have two packs, one for yourself and one for others. Tarot is your tool for spiritual growth and you need to keep it as closely connected with yourself as possible because other people have vibrations and energies that should not get connected with your personal cards. The same principle applies to your clothes or other personal things—you do not allow other people to use them, do you?

Myth #17: Tarot cards should not be left lying around.

I agree, of course, that Tarot cards should be cared for and treated with respect. It is not useful to dissipate the energy in the cards by leaving them around. Work with the cards only when you have the time and remember to wrap them up and put them back in your box when you need to do something else.

Myth # 18: Tarot cards should be kept wrapped in silk in a wooden box.

I actually agree with this. If you believe that it is your energy that gets invested in the cards, you need to know that positive energy has to be protected, not diluted. It is your spiritual tool and you need to keep it safe from negative energy. A purple or yellow silk cloth, which is nicely edged, acts as your altar cloth as well. A decorative wooden box kept in an uncluttered place where your personal, spiritual things are kept is advisable.

Myth #19: Addiction to Tarot is not healthy.

I tend to agree with this statement because no addiction is good. If you become too dependent on Tarot for everything then your personal initiative suffers. You need to be able to take your everyday life in your stride and consult Tarot only when it is required. However, you need to connect with the cards on a daily basis for meditation and healing purposes to generate specific energy in your life.

Myth #20: Taking the help of Tarot is a sign of weakness—only women resort to the cards.

What can I say to such an absurd statement? It is tantamount to saying that it is a sign of weakness to call a doctor when you are ill as you should suffer the pain and come out of it by yourself! Whatever helps you in the difficult business of living should be used and help should be sought from any source that offers it. Only the strong and wise have no qualms about seeking help. Clarifying your mind, connecting with your issues, understanding where you could be wrong and learning to rectify it cannot be a sign of weakness. Women are usually stronger than men when it comes to bearing stress, trauma and pain. A woman will go a long way to keep her family together, protect her children and ensure her happiness as well as theirs. Yes, Tarot is a 'woman's thing', but only because she is more open and willing to put aside her ego to try something that could help her.

Myth #21: Tarot should not be used during menstruation.

Doing certain things during menstruation is a cultural taboo in some societies. In India, we make much ado about menstrual cycles, but you should do what you believe in. If you believe in this kind of taboo, please do not touch the cards during menstruation. Admittedly I don't, since I am a product of this culture and believe in excercising caution. I read somewhere that at a vibration level, menstruation brings about some changes, but I am not sure what these changes are. If you really don't think it matters, then please follow what you are comfortable with. The only thing to be sure of is that you follow what you really believe in from the core of your being.

Chapter Two

The Major Arcana Cards

2.

The Major Arcana Cards

For any Tarot student, knowing the cards is of great importance. Understanding the symbols, the colours, the meanings and the implications is the basis for all Tarot work. The symbols and meanings do not have to be learned by heart. Just be aware of them and slowly, the cards will reveal their meanings to you as you grow in your work with Tarot. The shades of the meaning may vary but this is fine. Don't let it worry you, for it is your mind—with all its conditioning—that will be connecting with the cards. It is like getting to know someone. Gradually, you add new pieces of information about the person to the picture that you have in your mind. Over time, the picture enlarges and becomes more detailed. But, at times the unexpected behaviour of the person makes you wonder whether you really know him or her that well. You then become more aware of the personality traits and try to pick up tiny clues that may help you know the person better. It is the same with the cards. Treat them as people and let your acquaintance grow slowly but surely till they become your friends and reveal to you what you need to know. To aid this process of knowing, the information on each card has been divided into separate headings.

The **Voice** is the card revealing itself so that you see a different perspective of it.

The **Description** comprises of details, such as the symbols, colours, position, expression, associations and implications of the card that are important to understand.

Meaning is what the card usually and traditionally means.

Correspondence means the symbols and perspectives of other esoteric sciences that relate to Tarot (see the fourth chapter).

The Awakening explains what the card can awaken or bring to life in your mind.

The Shadow Aspect describes the negative implications of the card. As in a person, a quality that is positive, but not in balance, can have a negative implication. For example, too much ambition can become ruthlessness and excessive introspection can lead to inaction. Again, like a human being, there are some negative aspects of each card that need to be understood.

The Prayer to the archetype (represented by the figure on the card) is to understand the healing aspects of the card and to know that each archetype is an aspect of godliness. It also helps in understanding aspects of the self. The image needs to be examined along with the description so that it gets registered in the mind with the appropriate details. (You should use the prayer for the integration exercise given in the fifth chapter).

0
The Fool

0. The Fool

Voice

I am an original. I take risks and make you sample all aspects of life, even things that you are afraid of. So what if you have failed in the past? While there is life, there is hope. I am an optimist, and I make you see the bright side of things. I fear nothing. I will go out and live and act, not just sit or wait. I love life and all the uncertainties involved with this business of living. Sometimes I make foolish mistakes and take rash decisions. But life is a process of experimenting and learning. I will take the leap of faith. It does not matter if I land on my face. I will get up, go ahead and try again. I am innocent. I am happy, inexperienced and confident. Life is wonderful if you live in the moment and do not fret too much about the future.

Description

The Fool is depicted as a young person standing on a cliff, who is about to step off. He shows thc importance of the first step. He wears boots to signify that he is protected and deep down he understands his situation. He symbolizes life energy before it comes into manifestation (or fulfils its potential), which is infinite and can be given any shape. He faces northwest, the direction of the unknown and the unconscious. He will have to delve within himself and discover hidden knowledge. The sun behind him is shining and this indicates his optimism. The sun is still rising, which suggests that The Fool needs to grow and mature. It also shows his youth and his energy. His mantle is black, indicating ignorance and the wheels on the mantle symbolize the creative motion of the universe. He holds a long wand of magic and intuition and an empty bag to collect experiences and gain knowledge. The wand and the bag could also mean that he is carrying memories of past lives and instincts, the collective unconscious, which he will use on his way through life. He wears a green hat with a feather of an eagle, the favourite bird of Zeus, the Greek god, indicative of self-renewal and flight. The feather in his cap tells us that he has a positive, jaunty attitude towards his future. The colour green is the colour of growth. The sky is filled with the clear new light of spring. The head of the eagle on his knapsack shows us that he aims to soar high into the sky using his talents and skills, which means he has a desire to succeed. The white rose in his hand shows that he is peaceful with no malice in his heart. It also shows the purity of desire. The colourfully decorated tunic conveys his creativity, while the tattered sleeves convey an irreverent disregard for the norms of society. The white dog jumping and yapping at his feet stands for awareness, reminding him to curb his impetuosity while the snow-clad mountains represent the ambitious path that The Fool has to take and the goal that he has to reach.

Meaning

Symbolically, The Fool is forever new-born and about to begin his search for the Holy Grail. He sets out on his perilous journey, filled with hope and believing that anything is possible. Think of The Fool as a spirit facing unknown possibilities of self-expression as he enters the world as an innocent baby. He stands at a vantage spiritual height and is about to leap into manifestation. His journey will take him from ignorance to personal growth and spiritual evolution until he is liberated and merges once again with the divine. Like The Fool, we will confront and integrate the experiences and the challenges of life. The Fool of Tarot and the *atma* (soul) of Hindu philosophy are one, for both come into manifestation to experience the world and learn lessons and finally, to be liberated. Both are seeking enlightenment.

The Fool takes life as an adventure to be enjoyed. He inspires us to be open with others and with ourselves. He is a clown who can make fun of the powerful with impunity. He comes up with hidden truths that are revealing. The Fool reminds us that we may be taking our situation far too seriously and not seeing the potential for growth and insight.

The Fool is one of the most contradictory cards in the Tarot deck and adds energy and zest to any spread. On the surface, the card appears light and frivolous but deep down, it represents each one of us at every stage of life, no matter what age we are. All the challenges and new situations that life throws up makes us feel vulnerable and uncertain—just like The Fool.

The image of The Fool poised over a precipice conjures up the moments of fear, excitement and thrill that accompany every new venture. Each one of us is a Fool in our quest for the unknown. We act under his influence when we explore fantasies, and behave spontaneously, without malice.

The Fool is numbered zero which shows unlimited potential, the continuous circle of life, birth and death. It is the only card in the Major Arcana that features in regular playing cards (as the Joker).

Correspondences

The herb associated with The Fool is ginseng; the colour is pale yellow and the gemstone is tournamaline. The Fool is ruled by Planet Uranus, which governs independence, eccentricity, sudden flashes of intuition, freedom and inventiveness. The Sun sign Aries is associated with The Fool. It is the first sun sign and indicates a new cycle and the birth of a new year in which anything is possible. The rune (see the fourth chapter for an explanation of what runes are) associated with The Fool is Mannaz, the rune of mankind and awareness or Wunjo, the rune of joy. Both have some elements of The Fool.

The Awakening

Do not analyse things too much. Be like a child or you will never experience happiness. Be innocent and fun-loving. Sometimes you have to take risks. It is important that you live in the present with no regrets or anticipation.

The Shadow Aspect

The Fool indicates immaturity and foolish vices, a risk-averse nature and a disconnection with the child within you.

Other Decks

The Egyptian reference in the **Wirth deck** indicates that The Fool is the young Horus, the Egyptian deity, who later became the king after defeating the dark forces. As a youth, he had to hide from his wicked uncle Seth who had already killed his father, Osiris, and then wanted to murder him. In this card, Seth takes the form of a crocodile that gnaws his leg. This indicates opposition and an impulsive insistence to go forward despite existing problems.

The **Arthurian deck** depicts The Fool as the knight Parsifal (or Peredur, as he is known in the Welsh version of King Arthur's story). His mother did not want him to seek the Holy Grail and kept him dressed as a fool so that he would attract derision—but he persevered and became one of the finest knights.

The **Renaissance deck** depicts The Fool as Dionysus, the Greek god of ecstasy and light, who follows his own heart. The son of Zeus, the Greek god and Semele, a mortal, he is semi-divine and therefore, heroic. The Fool is dressed as a sixteenth-century court jester. He carries a staff decorated with grapes and a skull, which signify abandon.

Prayer

Oh Heavenly Father, allow me to experience the energies of The Fool and like him, let me walk in Thy divine grace without fear or shame. Make me as innocent as a baby and help me let go of my worldly fears. Let me act with the higher wisdom and see beyond appearances. Let me know that I am protected in Thy divine love, free to roam the world in Thy name and experience and learn all the lessons that are needed to liberate my soul. Reveal to me, my Father, the role that I must play.

I
The Magician

I. The Magician

Voice

I am the creative power of the universe, the master of the elements—air, water, earth and fire. I use them to convert ideas into realities. I see through problems and games that people play. I know how to get to the heart of the matter and resolve it through higher energy and attention. I can make anything happen. I may resort to a trick or two for I am The Magician. My magic wand is also the link with my higher self, which transforms and makes the impossible possible. I draw energy from above and apply it to the here and now. I give you the confidence for success. My energies guide you to realize your goals. My will power will bring you success and my discipline will bring you focus. Look to me to feel the power of the ego, the mastery of self that achieves, grows, lives and learns.

Description

The Magician is the bridge between the world of the spirit and the world of matter. His right hand holds a double-ended wand that is raised toward the sky and his left hand points to the earth. He is the transmitter of spiritual power, which he draws from above and manifests it on this earth. His magical table holds all four suits of the Minor Arcana, each representing an element: earth, air, fire and water. His robe is white, but his cloak is red, representing worldly experience and knowledge. He connects the conscious and the subconscious and suggests that all desires can become reality with the unity of both layers of the mind. The cosmic lemniscate or the figure-of-eight over his head symbolizes eternity and the interdependency of the spiritual and the material worlds. Around his waist, he wears an ouroboros (an ancient symbol in the circular shape of a serpent devouring its tail), which stands for transformation, shedding of the old and obsolete and the eternal circle of life. He stands against a yellow background of divine power and intellect. The wand also symbolizes the capability, talent and skill of The Magician. He can make anything happen. He suggests that determination is necessary for dreams to become reality.

The Magician is framed with red roses, symbolizing desires and the indulgence of the five senses. Those desires may be spiritual (fire), physical (earth), emotional (water) or mental (air) and he has the ability to bring them to fruition. The white lilies are indicative of spiritual thoughts, while the white band on his forehead indicates the activation of the third eye *chakra*, which results in intuition.

Meaning

The Magician is the male energy of aggression and pursuit that is required to initiate or start any venture. He does the magic that can transform the ordinary into the extraordinary by applying universal and natural laws to life. The Magician's function is to bring strength and power into our lives. Sometimes, he does this by questionable means for he could also be a trickster, a master Magician who could make you believe that the mud tiles that you are holding in your hand are actually gold coins. The Magician is the archetype of the active, masculine principle—the ultimate achiever who will do anything to get what he wants. He tells us that we have the ability to take the power of the universe and bring about the manifestion of our desires. He never makes an error of judgement. He is precise and exact and, therefore, performs tasks more efficiently than others. He is Hermes, the Greek god, and Thoth, the Egyptian god, the founder of occult sciences of magic, alchemy and astrology. He also resembles Apollo, the sun god, with his confident smile and shining eyes.

When you need to make things happen, turn to The Magician. He knows how to use all the tools at his disposal, to come up with clever plans that no one else would think of. He is strong-willed and rises to face any challenge head-on. The Magician is the card of capabilities and mental abilities. It is also an indicator of unseen powers, a sign that some magical influences could be coming into play in a person's life.

Correspondences

The Magician is associated with the colour yellow; the herb is oriental astragalus and the gemstone is Tiger's eye. The planet is Mercury. The rune associated with The Magician is Ansuz, which represents knowledge, skill, wisdom and communication.

The Awakening

You are capable of translating ideas into manifestations. Use your willpower to command the elements. Push yourself harder, to fully realize your desires by combining your intelligence, skills and aggression. Nothing is impossible for a Magician and you are one.

The Shadow Aspect

Weak or negative willpower can make you take short cuts, leading to corruption, inaptitude, indecision and sometimes, destructiveness. You could embark on a ruthless and amoral pursuit of success.

Other Decks

In the **Renaissance deck,** The Magician wears a winged hat and holds a snake-entwined staff. The Magician is a combination of Dionysus and Apollo.

Prayer

Oh Lord, I know that you are the magician of my life. Teach me Thy magic so that I, too, may transform my life from something ordinary to something extraordinary. Let miracles happen to me that will ease my burden and bring me joy. Give me your knowledge and let me face my challenges with equanimity and find solutions to the most difficult issues that weigh me down. Give me the courage, strength and power to change my reality and make all my dreams come true. Show me the ways creative power can function and how this world can be conquered by determination, will and magic. There is so much that I want to accomplish—let Thy divine strength flow within me and guide me to the right end.

II. The High Priestess

Voice

I am the unknown, the hidden, the eternal, the unconscious mind that you have forgotten and that you have searched for through centuries. To know my secrets, you will need to delve deep within yourself. Be a silent observer in the storms of your life and seek a balance between the extremes of black and white in this world. You will discover my scroll of eternal truths buried inside you only if you connect to your being. These are universal, moral and spiritual laws, secret arcane knowledge that can transform your life. I am the feminine principle, the virgin who still holds the mystery of existence within her. My ancient wisdom is for the initiate. I have been the keeper of records from time immemorial. I am the primordial memory that you can access. I am your guide to your dream world and to meditation. I lead you to deep wisdom and understanding of yourself. Look to me to lead you to the inner world. Remember, you walk this path alone.

Description

The High Priestess is the guardian of the great library of wisdom and knowledge. She sits between two pillars marked with the letters B and J. This alludes to the pillars in the Temple of Solomon and represents all the polarities of life. B stands for Boaz, signifying negation, while J stands for Jachin, meaning beginning. The lotus at the top of the pillars indicates the Egyptian belief that the world originated from water.The moon at her feet shows the power of the subconscious mind, the cycles of life and the ebb and flow of time and experience.

The High Priestess's robe seems to merge with water, an indication of the hidden knowledge that can emerge in the fluidity of our minds and consciousness. The scrolls that she holds in her hand contain the collective unconscious memory from the beginning of time. The scrolls have the word 'Tora' inscribed on them, which perhaps refer to the Torah, the Jewish books of laws. She wears a crown of moons, a full moon flanked by a waxing moon and a waning one, which associates her with the lunar goddess throughout the world. The moon rules the instincts, intuition, ebb and flow of moods and memories and childhood impressionability.

The High Priestess

Meaning

The backdrop cloth behind The High Priestess is embroidered with pomegranate and palm trees, indicating the integration of the male and the female to create immense possibilities. It also represents her virgin membrane, showing her as incorruptible to the temptations of the flesh, yet able to surrender to true love. The cloth leads to the deepest and the most esoteric secret knowledge. This indicates that The High Priestess can reveal strange hidden things. Like the moon on a dark night that lights up the path for a traveller, The High Priestess will help the querent to find his or her true path. The palms on the cloth mean fertility of the mind and the cube she sits on stands for the earth. The solar cross on her breast is a symbol of balance between male and female. In ancient Greece, it is an emblem of the four elements and in the Middle East it represents four directions and the four winds. The ancient Aztecs believed that a solar cross was a meeting place of the gods. The High Priestess wears this symbol on her heart, meaning that she connects with knowledge, and God. The unfolding mystery of life is the core of her knowledge. The High Priestess is Isis, the Egyptian goddess who sits at the portal before the great mystery of the universe. Her crown like the one that Isis wears. She sits between the pillars of Solomon's Temple, which means that she is the mediator of the spirit and matter.

The number II is the number of growth and harmony. It is a passive number, which reminds us of the vastness of our potential and the unlimited possibilities that we hold within ourselves. The High Priestess asks us to trust our intuition and the feminine aspect of our beings. Males need to connect to the feminine within them to enable their full growth and development or they will remain stunted and incomplete. For a woman, it means that she must trust her own instincts and the feminine principle.

The High Priestess can also represent a time of waiting and the need to strengthen oneself. She is the opposite of The Magician—she sits and is quiet and still while he stands and is loquacious and always moving. She is the moon goddess while he is the sun god. She also balances The Hierophant because she is his opposite—his knowledge is received, an external knowledge that is gained in society, while hers is intuitive. Being in a social context, his knowledge is handed down to be accepted as it has the stamp of authority, but her knowledge springs from within.

This card can also indicate a particular attraction to the occult, a thirst for secret knowledge.

Correspondences

The High Priestess is associated with the colour blue, the third eye *chakra* and the herb called cramp bark; the gemstone is moonstone. She is associated with the moon, and the rune of Lagus, which is feminine and relates to the moon, tides, water and creative potential and imagination or Kano, the rune for creative impulses, concentration, personal growth and new insights.

The Awakening

Her message is to go inward, to cultivate stillness, withdrawal and contemplation—to become aware of eternal connections and to use the insight gained from this connection with the inner self in everyday life.

The Shadow Aspect

The negative implications are sensual enjoyment without any depth and conceit, cunningness and guile. It means that you are not in touch with your inner being.

Other Decks

In the **Marseilles deck,** The High Priestess holds a book of mysteries in her hand.

In the **Visconti deck,** she is called The Papess or the female Pope.

Prayer

Oh Lord, let me be in touch with my being. Let me know who I am, what my destiny is, where I come from and where I will go. Teach me to be innocent and without guile, and to be truly open to eternal knowledge and the divine laws that govern us so that I may understand them, follow them and bring myself in balance with the universe. Reveal to me Thy secrets that will promote my growth. Let me be connected beneath this world of appearance to the source of my existence. Guide me to chart unknown territories of my mind and know and understand weaknesses and motives. Make me comprehend the hidden knowledge that will free me from all pleasure and pain and let me understand the true meaning of life and existence.

III. The Empress

Voice

I am the mother goddess who will fulfill all your desires. I am the abundance that you dream of. I will nurture and renew you. You know me as a giver, with unstinted compassion. I am the pleasure of the senses, the union of the outer and the inner being—the love that overwhelms you, that is all consuming—and yet I am above that ... I am the way to the infinite through physical, emotional and sexual means. I am the feminine principle, which is fertile. Come into my warm embrace and experience the beauty that the senses can produce. Merge with me and I will make you forget all constraints. I create wondrous things that remind you of their source and limitless supply. I am your imagination and creativity, pleasure and fulfillment. I invite you to reach your full potential by surrendering and submerging yourself to your passion. I have rich rewards for you—come and claim them.

Description

The Empress sits outdoors against a yellow sky, which represents creative intelligence. She is surrounded by a lush forest of cypress and other green trees, a flowing waterfall and ears of wheat suggestive of fertility, abundance and the subconscious connections with nature. The ears of wheat are sacred to Isis and the cypress trees are sacred to Venus, the Roman goddess of love. The waterfall to her left indicates her access to the unconscious mind as does the crescent on which she rests her foot. There is a cross at her heart *chakra*, indicating the union of the inner and outer aspect of being, of Shiva and Shakti. The idea that all creativity is based in the heart is indicated.

She wears a white robe of purity decorated with flowers and pomegranates that are symbols of the fertility of Venus. She holds the sceptre of life with a globe on the top, indicating that we create our own world. Her sceptre also shows her dominion over the created worlds. Where The High Priestess's dominion is over the inner world, The Empress has dominion over the world of the senses. The seven-pearl necklace is also a symbol of Venus, as are the myrtle leaves in the crown.

The Empress is full-figured. Below her couch is a heart-shaped pillow with the symbol of Venus emblazoned on it. The twelve pointed stars in

III
The Empress

her crown show her authority over the twelve signs of the zodiac and her reign over time.

Meaning

The Empress represents the powerful feminine force, the mother goddess of plenty who is eternally pregnant, hence always in the process of creation. The Empress is a creator, be it the creation of life, of romance, of art or business. While The Magician is the primal spark, the idea made real, and The High Priestess is the one who gives the idea a form, The Empress is the womb where it gestates and grows till it is ready to be born.

The Empress is the earth mother, the goddess of fertility. She is ruled by Venus, the planet of love, creativity, fertility, art, harmony, luxury, beauty and grace. She is associated with Demeter, the Greek goddess of harvests, Cybele, the Mediterranean earth mother, Ceres, the Roman goddess of agriculture and Lakshmi, the Hindu goddess of wealth.

The Empress and The High Priestess are the two aspects of the feminine archetype in the Major Arcana. The High Priestess symbolizes the dormant state of cosmic consciousness while The Empress represents the mind that has started the process of creativity and productivity. The coming together of The High Priestess and The Magician brings forth the warm and nurturing feminine aspect in the form of The Empress. She reigns over the bounty of nature and the rhythms of the earth. From her come all the pleasures and joys of the senses and the abundance of new life in all its forms. The Empress encourages you to strengthen your connections with the natural world. She unites The Magician and The High Priestess and brings action to dreams and ideas. Her generative forces help to bring creative, bright ideas to fruition.

Correspondences

The colour associated with The Empress is emerald green. Her herb is dong quai (the Chinese herb for women's ailments), the gemstone is emerald and the planet associated with her is Venus. The rune associated with her is Fehu, the rune of wealth and fulfilment.

The Awakening

Connect with the fertility and the abundance of Mother Earth. Be sympathetic and giving and you will receive plenty in return. Be aware of the aching beauty and creativity that is available to you.

The Shadow Aspect

The negative aspect of The Empress is feeling emotionally barren, living too much in the past, with old longings and unfinished business, destroying instead of creating, dependence on another person, excessive love of luxury and a dissipated lifestyle.

Other Decks

In the **Renaissance deck,** The Empress is depicted as Hera, the Greek goddess of women and marriage (and the wife of Zeus, Greek god of the sky and thunder), holding the celestial orb with a peacock above her. The myth associated with this card is that Hera asked her servant, the hundred-eyed monster Argus, to watch over Zeus to track his infidelity, but Hermes, the messenger god and son of Zeus, killed the monster at the behest of Zeus. Then Hera put the hundred eyes of Argus on the tail of the peacock and made the bird her associate in memory of her faithful servant.

Prayer

Oh Mother, let Thy abundance fill my cup and let Thy love flow through me so that I, too, may experience the wondrous world of the senses and create images of beauty and compassion in my life. Fill my senses with Thy grace, nurture and renew me and make me whole again. Take me in Thy warm embrace and show me the ways to fulfill my desires and yet be above them. Bring harmony in my life, and creativity and imagination. Plant seeds in me that grow into a luxuriant, lush forest of inner richness, of giving and caring. Let me know compassion and let my compassion reach all who need it. Let me be able to help in Thy work of making this earth a paradise of loving and giving.

יהוה
IV
The Emperor

IV. The Emperor

Voice

I am responsible for the well-being of my people and though sometimes I may appear distant, I have to be fair to all. I don't mind being unpopular for I stand for the moral and the ethical conduct or dharma. *I take hard decisions that no one else will take. Come to me when you are afraid of the storms and I will protect you. I have the mind of a scholar and discipline of a warrior, clarity of vision and courage of conviction. I may consult others but the final decision is always mine and I take it without flinching. I dislike battles and believe in negotiation but will wage a war if I need to. I am determined, tough and strong. I cannot be anything else, for my people depend on me. I will inspire you to be a leader, to live in this material world like a king. I will give you the ability to drill down to the core of things if you accept the responsibility for all your actions. I am at the heart of order, of rational approach and hard work. I can make a man out of you. The Empress is my woman and with her I create this world and teach you how to survive and how to live your life fully and successfully.*

Description

The Emperor complements the Empress. He is the masculine principle, the patriarch, the *raja* or king. He represents power and authority, and his sternness is very different from the beauty and the warmth of The Empress. Behind his throne are barren mountains, a symbol of the lofty heights of which he is the master.

The Emperor sits on a straightbacked stone throne, commanding and stately. His eyes meet ours directly. He is confident of his complete authority to rule. The Emperor represents structure, order and regulation—forces that balance the free-flowing, lavish abundance of The Empress. He advocates a stable, grounded world. He has no frills as he epitomizes gravity, simplicity and responsibility. He is stark and strong. He is the sky father (*raj pita*) as she is the earth mother (*raj mata*). The throne itself is decorated with four rams' heads, representing intellectual heights and sure-footedness in climbing the lofty crags. The four rams' heads and the orange background also indicate his vitality and sexual power. In his right hand he holds an Ankh, the key-shaped Egyptian symbol of life, and in his left hand is an orb representing the world over which he rules. The globe is also Mother Earth, the female sacred principle. It is only with the balance of spirit and matter—the male and female energies—that a strong reign is possible and The Emperor knows it. The Emperor is connected to Key XIII, the Death card through its cross-sum. He maintains his power through death and through his relationship with the other number thirteens, the queens of the Minor Arcana who support him. He wears armour but does not carry any weapons, which indicates that though he is capable of routing the enemy, he prefers to solve problems by negotiations that are fair and just. He is objective and makes decisions without an emotional bias, even if it means going against his own interest. He is a military strategist of great merit but uses force only as a last resort. He represents the moral and the ethical code. The Emperor has obtained his wisdom through experience, which is why his beard is white. He has fought wars and rules his people wisely.

Meaning

The Emperor is represented by number IV. It is a number of stability—there are four seasons, four elements, four rivers in the Garden of Eden and four sacred letters in the sacred name of God in Hebrew, YHWH, which stand for Jehovah. It takes tremendous energy to move the number. The strength of the Emperor lies in the stability he brings. His weakness invites the risk of stagnation and rigidity.

The Emperor stands for the domination of the material world, for authority, for paternity and regulation by law. He is the strong male energy that teaches us to use reason in handling our problems, to set limits, respect the society and its regulations, to pursue ambitions and achieve our goals with confidence and courage. His discipline leads to self-sufficiency.

The Emperor is connected to Zeus. He is the archetype of a father who makes all the rules, passes edicts and judgements and protects traditions and discipline. Together, the Emperor and Empress show the interdependence of opposing elements and how the balance of the opposing energies can provide the real solution to issues and problems that confront us.

Correspondences

The Emperor is associated with orange and red; the herb is ginger and the gemstone is ruby. The planet is Mars and the rune associated with him is Tiewaz, which represents stability.

The Awakening

The balanced objectivity of a leader is the hallmark of greatness. You are invited to be reasonable while in power and responsible for the well-being of others—how you use the power given to you is the test.

The Shadow Aspect

Trying to dominate will not get you anywhere. Rigidity, inflexibility and blindness to other points of view will cause stagnation. Intolerance and aggression are signs of weakness, while unruly behaviour and sexual aberration show a lack of control.

Other Decks

In the **Arthurian deck,** King Arthur is shown with Excalibur, his magical sword, across his knee. He was a champion of Christendom and of chivalry, and drew all the resources of his land to turn his kingdom into a land of great strength and vitality.

The **Wirth deck** features The Emperor seated on a cube emblazoned with a black eagle, suggesting the winning combination of matter and spirit.

Prayer

Oh Father, I know Thee to be all-powerful and strong. Let me experience these qualities in my life so that I too may emulate your example. Protect me and prevent me from taking wrong decisions. Teach me to negotiate moral dilemmas without flinching and to see my flaws objectively. Let me stand in the face of adversity and be unafraid of the storms of life. Let me be confident and brave, yet open to correction. Be there to hold me when I weaken and to guide me when I go wrong. Help me to be responsible for my actions and discern right from the wrong. Allow me to be receptive and recognize the rights of others so that I am fair to them. Inspire me to work hard. Inspire me to be determined and achieve my goals and overcome all obstacles in my path. Give me success, my Father, both internal and external, so that I, too, can live like a king.

V
The Hierophant

V. The Hierophant

Voice

Traditions and knowledge that have proved their worth emerge from me. I am the teacher who imparts knowledge and wisdom, the raj guru *who is responsible for guiding the king. My keys have unlocked doors for others before you and have given them the knowledge that has upheld many civilizations. I inspire you to pay heed to the external sources of inspiration as well. I endorse the organized methods of gaining knowledge and spiritual beliefs. I endorse the* guru–shishya parampara *(teacher–disciple tradition) and the conventional path. All the thinkers, thoughts and achievements down the ages that have been tested by time are dear to me like the knowledge of the Vedas, Puranas and the Upanishads. I urge you to set up high standards of behaviour, to gain the respect of your fellow human beings and garner the support of the society that you live in. Respect the outer aspects as much as the inner for the outer leads to the inner. Established religions, systems of philosophy, schools of thought, and organized systems of belief all teach you important lessons through me. I interpret divine knowledge and preside over ceremonies and rituals. My rituals will guide you to spiritual ends and my knowledge will bring you great regard from your fellow human beings. I connect the mortal to the divine.*

Description

The Hierophant in Greek means *the one who brings light*. The Hierophant is a vehicle for religious knowledge. He is the masculine counterpart to The High Priestess, but he differs from her. Whereas The High Priestess holds inner esoteric knowledge, The Hierophant is the keeper of recorded wisdom for the purpose of presentation. The Hierophant has an enormous responsibility because he stands as a religious icon. He is also known as The Pope who can dictate even to The Emperor. His right hand is raised in benediction and he channels his power through the society as the religions of the world.

His extended three fingers stand for the Holy Trinity—the Father, the Son and the Holy Ghost (or in Hindu terms, Brahma, Vishnu and Shiva). He is a religious figure in a formal church setting. He wears elaborate vestments, garments worn by priests in the medieval Church, of his office. He sits on a grey stone throne, indicating wisdom. There are four black and white circles at his feet representing the four cabalistic worlds—animal, vegetable, mineral and human.

The gold and silver crossed keys at his feet unlock the gates of heaven and hell. They also represent the inner and outer consciousness, the solar and lunar energies and all dualities that we need to resolve in life. Two priests with Franciscan tonsured haircuts kneel in front of The Hierophant. The robe of one priest is patterned with roses, which indicate earthly passion, while the other's robe has white lilies, signifying divine love and purified aspirations.

The Hierophant's task is to bring initiates into the fold of the Church so that they can take up their appointed roles. Besides churches, he presides over all groups and societies as his realm encompasses structured groups governed by rules reinforced by people with assigned roles. He emphasizes belief systems, facts, rules, procedures, and rituals.

This master of ceremonies wears a triple crown, symbolizing his wisdom in three spheres—the physical, emotional and intellectual. His staff also has a triple cross, reinforcing the same idea. The Hierophant sits between the pillars seen in The High Priestess card. Their colour is grey, indicating that their duality has been changed to inner neutrality and balance. He lives in the midst of the interplay of opposites without anxiety and inspires us to balance the spiritual and the material in our lives.

Meaning

The card represents the ruling power of religion. The Hierophant is a mediator between the spiritual and the worldly aspects of life. Through him, we participate in ceremonies and rituals. He endorses and interprets the meaning of institutions like marriage, society, family and traditions. He represents traditions, the orthodox, organized methods of nurturing spirituality and the received wisdom of the ages. Our ethical conduct and our code of behaviour are nurtured by him.

The Hierophant is similar to The Magician in that he also represents a link between us and the divine. Unlike The Magician who represents raw energy and is radical in his approach, The Hierophant is convention[al], a trusted guide who will take us by the hand and lead us to our spir[itual] goal. He is associated with hearing at a physical level and clairaudience (psychic hearing) at the spiritual level.

Correspondence

The Hierophant is associated with the colour orange-red, the gemstone emerald and the herb, sage. Number V is the number of the senses and the pain or physical suffering that come through them, testing a person's endurance. It needs control and balance to manage them, which the Hierophant provides. He is ruled by the zodiac sign of Taurus. The associated rune is Othila, which represents spiritual heritage.

The Awakening

Be alert and aware of how to sift the grain from the chaff with received wisdom. That is the sign of the times. Traditions and social values can comfort you in times of stress—do not underestimate them, but be aware of their limitations. The Hierophant is the representative of marriage and other social institutions. He connects to the power of the masses and has an ability to manage them. Education and learning are important to him.

The Shadow Aspect

Unconventionality and irresponsibility are the negative aspects and come with a price. It suggests ignorance which has no excuse and superstition that needs to be examined rationally.

Other Decks

In the **Renaissance deck,** the figure is shown holding a bishop's crook and a dragon, which together symbolize evil that is overthrown.

The **Visconti deck** shows The Hierophant as a wise old man, wearing a triple crown symbolizing the body, mind and spirit. Two fingers point towards the earth and two point upwards to the heavens, showing that both the worldly and spiritual aspects should be weighed.

Prayer

My Lord shows me the right way to live in this world that will lead me to peace and prosperity and to earn the respect of my fellow human beings. Let me understand others and know how to live together in a society. Let me follow the tried and tested methods and let me respect great men who can show me the right path. Be my guide and my teacher through this turbulent world. Let Thy knowledge and experience show me how to sift the grain from the chaff. Be my mediator and intercede on my behalf for the sins that I may have committed. Let Thy wisdom, experience and intelligence inspire and prevent me from making mistakes. Look after me and mine and shepherd me on the path of truth. Thy responsibilities are great, involving taking care of many human beings, not just of the exclusive few. Let me experience Thy grace.

VI
The Lovers

VI. The Lovers

Voice

We are the yin and the yang, prakruti *and* purush *(nature and consciousness), the conscious and the subconscious, the male and the female. All the polarities that exist are represented by us. We bring home the lesson that harmony between the inner and the outer being, between seemingly opposite sides, can only lead to inner growth and deliverance. There is always a choice regarding how you relate to the other and to the self. It is the complete union of Shiva and Shakti that creates their combined form, the* ardh-nareshwar, *which makes for wholeness. Realizing this is your release. The division is within yourself and you need to see it and integrate the opposing sides. Understand human existence. Where there is pleasure there will be pain; where there is love there will be hate, for the pendulum will swing in the opposite direction. Reconcile these opposites and accept both aspects. We also represent the sexual union of a male and a female and the natural attraction that can give great pleasure. We are the romantic dream that all lovers have. There are great lessons to be learnt through relationship, love and commitment. The ultimate union is between you and God and you need to recognize the seeds of godhood within you.*

Description

The Archangel Raphael, the angel of air and healing, is robed in fiery red and royal purple and presides over the lovers, showering benediction. The sun is shining brightly. They are in his care and protected for they are still innocent in their genuine love for each other, which is not corrupted. They are nude for they have nothing to hide. Is the angel arranging a marriage for them? The Lovers are Adam and Eve—Adam is the symbol of the conscious mind and the rational, while Eve is the symbol of the subconscious and the intuitive impulses. The man looks at the woman and the woman looks at the angel, signifying that the conscious mind connects with the subconscious mind, which has access to God.

There are two trees behind the figures. The branches of the Tree of Knowledge behind the woman bear the five apples of the five senses. The serpent of temptation entwines itself around the tree, signifying that the senses are easy to corrupt and a woman is a creature of the senses. Behind the male is the Tree of Life with twelve flaming leaves, suggesting the twelve signs of the zodiac. The flames behind the man represent the flames of passion.

It is important to eat the fruit of knowledge if one wants to pursue spiritual growth—it could lead to pain and banishment but the price of this choice has to be paid and is necessary for the growth and maturity of a person. In the myth of Adam and Eve, the eating of the apple brought about the downfall of the first human beings, but it also led to the rise of humanity. Karma led to suffering but expiation of the sin led to spiritual growth, which is the aim of existence.

Meaning

The cards depict the tension of opposite energies and the pleasure and pain associated with it. We have to find a balance. Resolving this duality is the greatest lesson and a resolution is possible only when we accept ourselves and the other person by recognizing each end of the spectrum. It shows personal choice; a deep, vital attraction and union between the male and female to perpetuate our world and take creation forward. It indicates all the myriad emotions, passions, reactions, experiences and understanding that are possible between man and woman. The Lovers represent perfection, harmony and mutual attraction. The card emphasizes finding your other self. It is about a soul-mate, perfect communication, about following an emotion that your soul needs. When this card appears, you are being told to trust your instincts. Whether it is a career choice or a person, take it, even if it seems difficult or irrational, for without it, you will never be complete. It indicates that the person you have a relationship with is the love of your life, so follow it. The choice may upset your well-laid plans but you still need to go with it if you want be true to yourself.

The choice could have a moral undertone. Your value system is tested and challenged and the path you choose will reflect your inner truths. The choices are never really easy or obvious either. Unlike The Fool's choice, which has no right or wrong answers, the choice of The Lovers is tricky because a wrong choice could lead you down the wrong alley.

The mountain in the background is a male phallic symbol, while the water is a feminine symbol, indicating a balance between the two. The number VI represents the balance of opposites. The earth beneath the feet of The Lovers is green and fertile, indicating life and happiness and the coming together of romantic love, passion and sex in harmony and companionship.

The card of The Lovers is connected with Key XV, The Devil card, by cross-sums, which shows the distortion that could occur in a man–woman relationship and all the attendent negative elements.

Correspondences

The card of The Lovers is associated with the colour orange, the herb, parsley, the gemstone rosequartz, the sun sign Gemini and the planet Mercury. Since it is a dual sign, the Lovers are able to see both sides of a situation. Number VI stands for reciprocation, adjustment, union and mutual exchange. The rune associated with the Lovers is Gebo, which is connected to marriage.

The Awakening

The choice is about how well you connect with the two aspects of yourself—the outer being will reflect the inner you. All your romantic decisions are based on this inner harmony, which should be recognized.

The Shadow Aspect

Disharmony and wrong choices, infidelity and sexual excesses constitute the dark side of The Lovers. Something within you needs to change—examine it, acknowledge it and stabilize your emotions.

Other Decks

The **Renaissance deck** depicts The Lovers as Cupid, the Roman god of love, and Aphrodite, the Greek goddess of love, beauty, and sexuality, demonstrating the coming together of the power of love and beauty and their impact on human beings.

The **Mythic deck** refers to the judgement of Paris (of Troy) where he gives the coveted golden apple to Aphrodite in a contest between her,

Athena and Hera, which led to the Trojan War. This story highlights the issue of choice.

The **Wirth deck** shows a choice between being a virtuous woman or a promiscuous one. Though simplistic, the important point is that all choices have consequences that are far-reaching, which means that it is wiser to seriously consider and weigh the pros and cons before making any choice.

Prayer

Oh Lord, I have many choices in front of me and I do not know which the right one is or what the consequences of the choice will be. Help me, my Father, to see the truth and make the right choice based on the right values and judgement. Temptations are many and it is so easy to get misled. I know that life is full of contradictions and yet, there is unity beneath these differences. Let me see the oneness beneath the surface so that I can connect with it. Show me the harmony in the opposites and the humility to reconcile them for Thy glory. Show me the path of true love and the openness to see Thy presence in the person as well as in my own being. Let me be fair, balanced and faithful in my commitment and take forward Thy work in this world. Protect me, Father, from quarrels, infidelity and unstable emotions and lead me to myself and Thee through my relationships.

VII
The Chariot

VII. The Chariot

Voice

I am the victorious warrior returning home. I have fought many battles and won them all. The sky is the limit for me and I never give up in the face of opposition, adversity or difficulty. You use my energies when you fight till the end. I can teach you how to succeed and win provided you are willing to stake everything on your victory. I am not for the faint-hearted. The sphinxes that pull my chariot are within my control and I use them to give me different views as they are black and white, representing polarities. I bring you the strength to proceed with focused determination and use your aggression for achievement and glory. I can give you the power to accomplish what you want, to achieve your goals and desires. You need to have discipline, persistence and the ability to work hard. I am Arjuna who has pierced the eye of the fish and won Draupadi. I have spent eons working on my weaknesses and overcoming them. My mastery is over myself, which is the greatest victory of all. My clarity of thought, self-confidence and single-minded efforts have brought me where I am and my will is my greatest triumph. Depend on me to shape you, mould you and make a winner out of you.

Description

The Charioteer has triumphantly left the conquered city behind to pursue new conquests and adventures. He is bold and unafraid with the supreme self-confidence that comes from fighting many wars. He is emblazoned with astrological symbols and talismans of ritual magic on his person. He wears a laurel wreath of victory, indicating that victory comes from self-control and emotional stability. The two crescent moons on his shoulders are Urim and Thummim, one with a smiling face and the other with a sad expression, indicating that the inner balance of emotions is necessary for a warrior. They also show different aspects of the moon and The Charioteer's control over his emotions, be it pleasure or pain. If he is fearful or imaginative—that is, affected by the phases of the moon—he cannot be a true victor, for the real victory is when emotions and passions are controlled. The blue canopy with its bright stars suggests the influence of celestial cycles. He holds a staff of authority in his right hand, which bears a crescent and a figure-of-eight, the symbol of eternity. It shows that the conscious personality must work in conjunction with the subconscious to win. He uses his dominant consciousness and purposeful concentration to control his sphinxes. He needs no reins to control them as his control comes from his mind. The black sphinx represents severity or suffering while the white sphinx represents mercy and joy. Both have to be in balance for a true conqueror, for only then can the battle of life be won.

The sphinxes are portrayed with human heads on animal bodies, suggesting that only the evolution of consciousness can free a person from the yoke of circumstances. The winged solar disc links him to the Egyptian gods; the chariot is the vehicle of the spirit and The Charioteer is the lord of light. The Hindu *lingam* in a *yoni* suggests the reconciliation of opposites. The chariot's yellow wheels have emerged from the deep water of the unconscious energy, suggesting that illusion needs to be conquered by conscious thought. The four pillars supporting the canopy represent the control of the four elements and the stability of the rider who is grounded with the power of number four. The Charioteer's diadem has at its centre, an eight-pointed star which will be seen again in Key XVII, The Star. It symbolizes his dominion and the beginning of spiritual power and energy. The square pendant that he wears on his heart *chakra* indicates the earth element that keeps him grounded in reality. He wears armour like The Emperor's. His will, knowledge and intention are in perfect balance.

Meaning

The card of the Chariot represents the positive aspects of the ego. Success comes from beating the competition to become number one. Such moments are glorious in the right circumstances. Trouble and turmoil will be conquered through your confidence and control. This is an important card for disabled people, advising them that a successful life can be built up within the limitations imposed on them, if they want it enough. Aggression can be very destructive, but it is also a powerful energy that can be channelled creatively.

The Charioteer wears emblems of the sun, yet the planet associated with this card is the moon. The Chariot is all about motion, and yet it is often shown as stationary. On the one hand, the card of The Chariot indicates loyalty, faith and motivation, but on the other hand, it can also signal a ruthless desire to win. The most famous charioteer is Krishna, the Hindu god, who in the Bhagavad Gita drove Arjuna's chariot and illuminated his mind with his discourse.

The Chariot card is related through cross-sums (the sum of the digits) to Key XVI, The Tower. Some authorities say that The Charioteer is the god of spring, the son of the queen of heaven as indicated by the circle of the zodiac in his belt. He channels energy from the universe through the eight-pointed star on his brow, representing Venus, and brings it to the earth below, signified by the square on his chest. The four corners of the earth are represented by the four poles of the canopy. The charioteer is a true conquered because he has conquered himself and his weaknesses.

Correspondences

The Chariot card's colours are blue and yellow and the herbal correspondence is the dandelion; the gemstone is amber. It is governed by the moon. Number VII indicates victory and conquest (the Book of Genesis in the Bible states that God rested on the seventh day after creating the universe). The rune associated with The Chariot is Ehwaz, which represents journeys and Kano, which signifies fire and inner light.

The Awakening

Conquering yourself is important for you to gain a victory over the external world. Goals will be achieved by single-minded concentration and efforts. The world awaits your triumph.

The Shadow Aspect

Look at your weakness and lack of will. If you find short cuts, your inner growth will be compromised. Unethical victory is no victory.

Other Decks

In the **Renaissance** deck, The Charioteer is depicted as Mars, the Roman god of war. He had a long-standing love affair with Venus because of his sex appeal and produced Harmonia, the Greek goddess of concord, indicating that the combination of love and passion will produce harmony. The energy of Venus in The Lovers' card is gentle and beautiful while that of Mars in The Chariot card is courageous, positive and vigorous. The need for balance, however, is vital.

The Wirth deck shows the sphinx as represented in the Greek myth of Oedipus, the king of Thebes. The sphinx was a deadly creature that seized young men and demanded correct answers to its riddles and killed them if they failed to do so. The card of The Chariot suggests that we must solve the riddle of our life or be overwhelmed by it.

Prayer

Oh Lord, I know that I am weak and limited, confused and fearful. I need Thy grace to make me see my goals and Thy strength to help me conquer the self. Let me rise in this world and realize my ambitions. Show me ways of controlling and understanding my emotions so that I can see the reality of existence. Let me not baulk at self-discipline and all that needs to be done to make me face my adversaries. Dear Lord, give me the courage, determination and the will to follow Thy path and lead me to victory. Direct me to master myself to accomplish my hopes, dreams and expectations. Let me win this battle of life and fulfill Thy mission.

VIII
Strength

VIII. Strength

Voice

I have faced my beast and so can you. It is not as frightening or difficult as it seems. Follow me to know how to tame the wildness within you and to understand the nature of the beast within. There is no great secret in doing what I do. If you have faith in divine protection—which is always there with you—then there is no fear. Your fears are doubts and uncertainties about God. Realize that and you will be free. Neither condemn nor ignore your animal nature—just accept it, observe it and let it transform itself for a higher purpose. Do not avoid what seems dangerous but face it. Look the beast in the eye and see it wilt. Expand your awareness, know your strength and love others without any ulterior motive. Endurance is necessary for all growth, so surrender and accept yourself. You may have to go through pain but that is fine. When I love, I encourage and recognize the best in my partner. In my relationships, I acknowledge the other person fully. I am in charge of soul development. I can teach you to create the person of your dreams, a soul-mate made by the power of love.

Description

An innocent maiden is robed in white with a garland of red roses and she looks lovingly at the orange lion who seems to be licking her hand. She has flowers in her hair too, and she is either opening or closing the mouth of the lion. The lion holds no terror for the maiden. On the contrary, the lion is surrendering to her. She has no magic wand but a figure-of-eight (lemniscate) over her head indicates divine protection, which she is sure of. Her faith is reflected on her calm countenance and the ease with which she handles the lion. The lion is depicted in orange as a symbol of fierceness, primal instincts and masculine will.

The garlands of roses stand for desires, indicating that all humans have desires and that is acceptable. What is needed is to balance desires with divine surrender and live fully without fear in this world. Her crown of flowers indicates creative imagination while her white gown signifies her purity.

Meaning

There are two main themes in this card. There is strength—both of the physical body and the inner being—and the ability of each person to tame the beast within. It is also a card of courage and energy. It represents both the lion's pulsating, roaring energy and the maiden's steadfast will. The innocent maiden is unafraid, undaunted and indomitable. In some Tarot decks, she opens the lion's mouth, in others, she closes it. Either way, she proves that inner strength is more powerful than raw physical strength. It is a card about anger and impulse management, about creative answers, leadership and maintaining one's personal honour. It can also stand for a steadfast friend.

This card represents strength, determination, and power in a manner similar to The Chariot. However, the differences are obvious. Instead of a powerful, focused warrior, we encounter a gentle woman, unarmed and without the protection of any armour. She overcomes the lion with a quiet strength that comes from within. Where The Charioteer represents outer strength and will, the card of Strength signifies inner power, the power of the human spirit to overcome any obstacle. Standing unprotected in an open green field, the maiden represents the spirit.

The maiden is an extension of the previous cards featuring women: The High Priestess, who represents the subconscious and intuition, and The Empress, who stands for the senses and creativity. She is willing to engage with life and creatively find ways of controlling, directing and managing the beast. She is the feminine, watery, passive principle while the lion represents the male, positive, active principle initiated by The Magician. The blue mountain in the background is the same phallic symbol seen in The Lovers' card. The lion is a symbol of our animal passions and desires.The maiden's will is her desire for right action. She knows her powers and applies certain rules of life to combat the challenges of life. Life is her teacher and she seeks infinite laws to guide finite actions.

Strength or fortitude is a cardinal virtue. It hints at physical as well as inner strength. The contest between man and beast is represented in this card, which also signifies the energy of quiet determination. Strength is not a flashy card, but one that is solid and reliable. It also stands for patience and compassion. Getting angry is easy when circumstances turn sour, but dealing calmly with frustrations takes great strength. Accepting others and forgiving mistakes also requires great inner strength. We need strength to mould situations gently. The Chariot controls through mastery and authority, but the Strength card is more subtle, even loving, as depicted in the picture, which shows the lion being guided and tamed by the maiden's gentle hands.

The Strength card was originally named Fortitude and is accompanied two of the other cardinal virtues in the Major Arcana—temperance and justice. The meaning of Fortitude was different from the interpretation of this card. It was about moderation in one's attitude while dealing with pain and accepting it in a stoic way.

The Strength card encourages us to get in touch with our desires and create a harmonious union between the conscious, rational aspect of our nature and our subconscious, intuitive side. Strength is associated through the cross-sums with The Star. The Star of Bethlehem guided the wise kings to Baby Jesus, which indicates the results the card of Strength can bring and the beauty of life thereafter. Number VIII also has strong Buddhist connotations indicating the eightfold path that leads to a happy and fulfilled life

The card tells us that any situation that appears challenging has a spiritual aspect. The problem can be solved if we change the terms of reference and see situations and relationships in a new and more loving context. The Fool on his journey of life, learns self-discipline and courage.

Correspondences

The colour of the card is yellow, the herb is cayenne and the gemstone is cetrine. The card of Strength is associated with the sun sign Leo and there is a connection with the heart *chakra.* The runes that represents the card of Strength are Thyrisaz, which stands for protection, Uruz, the rune for health and strength and Wunjo, which signifies joy and hope.

The Awakening

There is no fear if you realize the power of spiritual protection. You can conquer any obstacle with this knowledge because you will have all the strength that you need. Be aware of your power and be secure in this knowledge. Faith and belief, endurance and patience are your greatest strengths.

The Shadow Aspect

This indicates that the physical and material dominate the spiritual. It shows weariness, lack of faith and a weak moral fibre.

Other Decks

In the **Renaissance deck,** the Strength card is shown as Heracles, the Greek mythic hero (also known as Hercules in Roman mythology) fighting the ferocious Nemean lion, which was protected by its golden fur. Heracles, being the son of Zeus, the supreme Greek god, is an archetype of strength. He is a hero associated with the sun, as shown by the twelve archetypal labours, each one standing for a specific zodiac sign. The myth is that being an illegitimate child of Zeus, Heracles attracted the anger and jealousy of Hera, one of Zeus' wives, who sent various obstacles in Heracle's path. The twelve labours of Heracles included killing the Nemean lion.

The **Wirth deck** shows a woman calmly dealing with a fierce-looking lion. Her floppy rimmed hat forms the figure-of-eight.

Prayer

Fill my life with Thy strength, oh Lord, so that I can tame my inner beast. My weaknesses have different guises and I don't know how to tackle any of them. Without your help, I will not be able to control and overpower them. Teach me, oh Father, to have faith in you and to trust in Thy infinite support. My doubts in you make me vulnerable to all the negativity that is present around me. Let me feel Thy protection and Thy love constantly so that I too, may extend that love to others. My selfishness and self-love prevent me from giving myself freely and completely. Give me the endurance to face the trials of my life without flinching and the patience to understand Thy divine will.

IX
The Hermit

IX. The Hermit

Voice

I bring you the light of wisdom. I am an expert that you always need, a counsellor, a teacher who will show you the right path. I know what it is to live in this world, which is filled with unhappiness and travail. I have a solution for you but you must follow me with your heart and soul. I will not give you any answers but will teach you how to find them. Look within yourself for all the answers are there. Connect with your being and unravel all your problems through your subconscious mind. You need patience and contemplation, sincerity and commitment, and above all, the objectivity to acknowledge the truth without flinching. If you will promise me these qualities, I will promise to walk with you all the way and illuminate your path with my light of knowledge and experience. Do not feel lonely for we are all alone on this spiritual journey. All your attachments are for here and now—your success, your relationships, your money, name and fame will disappear with the setting sun. I will be there for you even when these temporary things leave you, to hold your hand and to take you to the height of spiritual understanding and to the love that is eternal and true.

Description

The Hermit stands alone on a mountain-top, lantern in hand, awaiting seekers of knowledge. The Hermit has attained his spiritual pinnacle and is ready to share his knowledge. He is far above the weary climbers, for whom he lights the way. His lantern is a six-pointed star or the seal of Solomon (the magical ring or protection seal of the Biblical King Solomon). This is the lantern of truth. It is the divine focal point and the spark of divinity in all of us. He carries a yellow staff of intellect and higher knowledge as he stands on this narrow path of initiation. His cloak is a mantle of discretion and, in some decks, he covers the lantern partially with his cloak, protecting the truth from profane eyes. He is ready to help anyone who asks for light. He has travelled the road many times and knows what pitfalls are to be encountered, an experienced guide as indicated by his white beard. His grey robe indicates the resolution of the opposites in his life. His hooded cloak of contemplation envelops the knowledge of ages. He remains on the mountain throughout the night of spiritual darkness. He represents the idea that ultimately, we are all alone, particularly in our quest for the divine. Only those who are humble can see the light of the Hermit's lamp for others are too blinded by the ego to see anything beyond themselves. The snow at his feet represents the height of spiritual attainment.

Meaning

The Hermit stands for absolute wisdom, the goal of existence. The bearded ancient looking down at night signifies accomplishment, wisdom and the attainment of goals, as well as the search for truth. Number IX is the number of pure intellect. It is also a number of initiation, in which all the numbers are gathered, after which a new cycle starts from number X. The Hermit's body, too, is shaped like the numeral of nine (9).

The Hermit has not escaped reality to hide in the mountains. He is somebody who has gone through life and learnt its lessons. He knows that however different one individual is from another, all of us have to ultimately take the spiritual journey and that the end of all life is death. The Hermit represents the desire to turn away from the distractions of the everyday world in order to focus on the inner world. He seeks answers within and knows that they will only come with quiet and solitude. Sometimes we come to a point in life when we begin to question the obvious and we need to search for inner realities. This search is mainly a solitary quest because the answers do not lie in the external world, but within us.

The Hermit often suggests a need to spend time alone, a period of reflection. During times of activity and action, he stands for the still, silent centre that must be created for balance. He can also stand for guidance from wise teachers. When you are involved with any serious pursuits, The Hermit can be the guide to show you the right direction. Meditation, contemplation, self-examination and the re-evaluation of life's goals are important aspects of The Hermit.

The Hermit is the wise spirit within. He, like the Fool, stands at the edge of a precipice on the peak of a barren mountain. But unlike the innocent, naive Fool who carelessly steps over the edge, The Hermit holds the staff of wisdom in one hand and a light in the other to give directions to those who do not know the way. The Hermit is the ancient spirit that lives within us through the existence of the collective unconscious, the universal mind which guides us through the darkness with its clear light. He does not have much to say in the form of words. He silently shows the way with his light.

The Hermit helps others with love, compassion and detachment. He is not critical and is able to see the varied paths people choose for themselves to reach the divine. He does not need to convince others of what they should do. However, there are times when The Hermit can represent spending too much time alone, excessive isolation, literally becoming a hermit and cutting oneself off from human contact.

Correspondences

The astrological correspondence for this card is the sun sign Virgo, characterized by a detail-oriented nature, strong analytical faculties and perfectionism. The Hermit is associated with the colours grey and yellow-green and the gemstone, topaz. The herb is liquorice. The rune that represents The Hermit is Algiz, the rune for divine power, or Perdhro, which is associated with mystery. Meditating on this archetype teaches you to honour the wisdom within yourself.

The Awakening

There is wisdom within you if you allow it to flower. You do not need the trappings of society. You can be alone, yet not lonely. Your light can illuminate the world.

The Shadow Aspect

The Hermit indicates foolishness and emotional immaturity; also, being hasty, impulsive, careless, imprudent and unnecessarily cautious or fearful.

Other Decks

In the **Renaissance deck,** The Hermit is associated with the Greek legend of Kronos, the father of Zeus, who ate his own children.

In the **Wirth deck,** The Hermit is shown with a serpent at his feet. Serpents indicate wisdom and renewal as they regularly shed their skins.

Prayer

I am so enmeshed in this world that I forget that this is just a transient sojourn. I suffer but I am unable to find solutions to my suffering. Oh Father, I know that truth is a lonely path and that we must all walk alone. Give me the courage and understanding to see this truth. I long for Thy light that will illuminate my dark night of the soul. Relieve my soul of all its pain and guide me to Thee. Give me the patience and commitment to tell right from wrong. Be my guide and take me through this uncharted sea of life by holding my hand and showing me your light.

X
R
A
Wheel of Fortune

X. The Wheel of Fortune

Voice

I am the Wheel of Life that has no beginning and no end. My perpetual motion brings change. I make you realize that nothing is permanent in life. If you keep moving with me you can be happy. You can go beyond time with total inner awareness, for then you will be at the centre of my wheel and stop spinning. That is the state of meditation or stithipragya, *which is the aim of all human life. Be like the blue sphinx who sits on the top of my wheel and become the observer of life. My change is within the fixed laws of the universe that no one can challenge. Expect the unexpected and look for patterns and clues to understand the nature of life. Everything that goes up will come down, just as everything that goes down will come up. Know this and live by it, for it will make you less attached to pleasures—for no pleasure is eternal. Time will take it all away—so honour time. Let go of your ego. I will bring you luck, if you will let me, for it is up to you to take advantage of the right opportunity that I offer. Finally, it is you and you alone who is the master of your destiny.*

Description

There are three concentric circles in the card of The Wheel of Fortune, representing the will, love and creation. The outer circle represents the material world, the middle circle is formative power and the inner circle is the creative force. The same symbolism is seen in the three tiers of the Hierophant's crown. In the outer circle are the letters making up the word 'rota', which means the wheel. It could also be the word Tora or sacred knowledge (*orat* in Latin), an oracle. This is interspersed with the Hebrew letters *Yod Heh Waw Heh* (YHWH) of the Tetragrammaton, the sacred name of God. Together they make the universal creative process. The wheel with eight spokes is the eight-pointed star in Key XVII, The Star, indicating eternal energy. The Wheel of Fortune represents the laws that govern human existence and the constant flux of time.

Descending on the left side of the wheel is Typhon, the Greek angel of death, and ascending on the other side is Anubis, the jackal-headed Egyptian god and protector of life, indicating that both life and death are aspects of our existence. The blue sphinx on the top represents the detached outlook that should be the aim of life. It has a man's sword of toughness and discrimination held over the female breast, which symbolizes compassion—both male and female qualities are required. The blue sphinx has conquered its animal instincts and has human intelligence as portrayed by its animal body with a human head. It has reconciled the opposites and exists in the state of *sakshi bhav* (detached observation) as an observer of life. He watches the spectacle of life go by without being affected by it. That is the secret of happiness and the way to live in this world.

The symbols in the middle circle are the alchemical elements of air, fire, earth and water—mercury, sulphur, water and salt. The blue background of the card represents wisdom. In the clouds shown at the four corners are four fixed signs of the zodiac—Taurus, Leo, Scorpio and Aquarius—which represent the unchanging laws of the universe in which The Wheel of Fortune rotates. These are the four fixed signs of the zodiac, but they all have wings, signifying movement and change within a fixed context. The book they are all reading is the Torah, which represents wisdom. The four animals represent the four elements: earth, fire, water and air.

Meaning

The Wheel of Fortune teaches us endurance and fortitude, to keep our balance in the midst of the fluctuations of time. The Wheel of Fortune is one of the few cards in the Major Arcana that does not have a human figure as a focal point. This is because its centre is above the realm of man. Tarot recognizes that each person sets his own path in life, but is also subject to the larger cycles of change that include nature and other cosmic aspects. The card indicates the changes that takes place in life. If the card is upright, the changes will take place to your advantage because the card is associated with success and working in harmony. It indicates a force propelling you forward towards harmony and luck. The new beginnings in the cycle are also indicated.

Correspondences

The colour for The Wheel of Fortune is purple; the herb associated with it is the slippery elm and the gemstone is sapphire. The planet associated with this card is Jupiter, the planet of opportunity, growth, success and expansion. The rune is Jera, which is associated with the seasons of the year and the cycles of rebirth. The number X is a higher octave of the number I and in this context, the rune is Raido, which is related to inner journeys.

The Awakening

Flux is the reality of existence—what goes up must come down. Take the detached position of the blue sphinx and be an observer of life, so that you will come to the centre of the wheel of time and become still.

The Shadow Aspect

Resisting the cycle of time will not get you anywhere. Procrastination, feeling helpless or fighting change are indicated. Luck may not be on your side—extra efforts may be required and the consequences of wrong decisions have to be faced.

Other Decks

The **Renaissance deck** shows the Roman belief that human life is governed by the whims of Fortuna, the goddess of fortune, who is shown standing before the wheel, which symbolizes the various stages of life. She points to a castle on her right and an abyss to the left.

The **Morgan Greer deck** connects the card with the virtue of prudence, which according to Cicero, the Roman philosopher, had three aspects: memory, intelligence and foresight. Together they provide an understanding of the past, present and future.

Prayer

Teach me to let go, Father. Stay by my side when the going is tough. It is so painful to accept change and so much more comfortable to continue on the same track. My life is filled with ups and downs. I swing like a pendulum. Help me to find my balance not only when I am down but also when things are looking up—for that is the time when one gets misled by the false sense of the self. Let me become an observer of life like the blue sphinx. Let me flow with time and do away with fears and insecurity in the face of uncertainty and flux. Let me have faith in Thee and accept whatever comes to me in good grace. Let me understand the transience of time and uselessness of clinging to the past. Teach me acceptance and courage and let me live in Thy divine grace in humility and faith.

XI
Justice

XI. Justice

Voice

I am the power that makes you decide what is right and what is wrong. I stand firm by the truth in any circumstances and would advise you to do the same for finally, truth will prevail. See me operate slowly but surely. Justice may take time but it will be served. Whatever a man sows, he will reap. That is a universal law and no one can escape it. The truth is usually between the two extremes and you need to discover that for yourself. Make your choices with care as you are responsible for the consequences of your decisions. My sword of discrimination will cut away all pretences, exposing the core of reality. My scales teach you evaluation and being fair. Be ethical in your principles and moral in your action. Let wisdom and mercy come together in all your judgements. Understand that the mark of a true man is his integrity and his respect for the rights of others. I am fearless for I have done no wrong and can look in the eyes of any man or beast. You, too, can become like me if you walk my path. It is a difficult road and less travelled as only the truly great have the courage to face themselves. In the end, it is only they who win the game of life.

Description

The figure of Justice is seated in front of two pillars, with a cloth stretched in between like that in the card of The High Priestess. The pillars extend beyond the card to indicate that the play of cosmic justice does not ever stop. The right pillar symbolizes mercy, while the left one stands for severity. The number of the card—the numeral of eleven (11)—is reflected in the position of the two pillars.

Justice sits between the two pillars, emphasizing that balance is the hallmark of judgement. Evaluation, an important part of Justice, is expressed by the scales in the left hand of the figure. Since she is the personification of spiritual justice, she wears no blindfold. Her crown has three turrets, representing knowledge, argument and decision. She wears two square jewels, one at the Agya *chakra* or third eye *chakra* and the other at the Anahat *chakra* or the heart *chakra*, indicating that all decisions must be made by using wisdom, in this sense, a combination of justice and mercy. In her logical right hand is a double-edged sword of decisiveness and discrimination that cuts through illusion and indicates that logic is necessary to dispense justice as is intuition, which is suggested by the golden scales in the intuitive left hand. She wears a slipper of understanding, which is visible. She is stern, unflinching and fearless, ready to take on the world for the cause of righteousness. Her posture and demeanour indicate a no-nonsense approach. She is here to expose the truth and bring to light those issues that require our attention.

Justice sits on a stone throne of wisdom. The colour of the throne is grey, indicating a neutral perspective. She wears a scarlet robe, the colour of passion and courage, while the green cape represents creativity and growth. The cloth draped behind the figure is purple, signifying divine wisdom and confidence. The colour lets us know that we are in the presence of the highest court of divine justice, while the yellow behind the cloth is the higher consciousness, the source of true knowledge.

Meaning

The Justice card's prime message is that of accountability. The card is straightforward and to the point. There is no hiding, no making excuses and no procrastination. There is a serious feel to this card, like the tone of the courtroom. It refers to legal matters of all kinds, but is not restricted to them.There is a similarity between The Emperor and Justice. Both cards stand for universal order, The Emperor in its underlying structure and Justice, in the action of karma or cause and effect.

Justice often appears when you are concerned with doing what is right. This card can also appear when you are feeling the impact of a past mistake or a good deed. The cause you set in motion at one time is now returning to you as an effect. Sometimes Justice is a signal to do what needs to be done. A time comes when responsibilities must be accepted, and accounts settled. The past will continue to haunt you if you do not recognize your mistakes and make amends for them. You will need to weigh matters carefully and perhaps, make important decisions about your future course.

The card indicates that you have just completed a cycle of destiny and a brand-new cycle is about to commence. We move from the physical world of the first ten cards of the Major Arcana, which represent development, to the next ten cards, suggesting an entry into the metaphysical world where development accelerates and lessons have to be learned. It symbolizes both karma and *sanskara*, action and conditioning. In practice, the Justice card symbolizes the laws of karma and the judicial system.

In many Tarot decks, Justice is given the number VIII, which was considered the number of divine justice by the Greek philosophers Aristotle and Plato. This is because number VIII can be divided into two equal parts of four, which is the number of the cardinal virtues: justice, prudence, temperance and strength.

Correspondence

The colour of the Justice card is green; the plant is plantain and the gemstone is bloodstone. Justice is ruled by Libra. The runes associated with this card are Thyrisaz, the powerful rune of protection or Nauthiz, which gives the courage and wisdom to decide what to do in a complex situation. The number XI is a higher octave of the number II and connected to The High Priestess. Unlike the hidden knowledge of The High Priestess, Justice is decided in the open. Justice is also connected to Key XX, Judgement, which also deals with knowing, learning, experiencing and accepting the truth.

The Awakening

Justice will be served and divine Justice is perfect. You will get what you deserve. Know this and live by it. Justice assists you in breaking through the veils of illusion or deception. This archetype helps you achieve and maintain balance in all aspects of your life.

The Shadow Aspects

You see the biased mind, dishonesty in yourself and others. It also represents injustice, inequality and legal complications, indicating that you should use mercy and understanding when judging others.

Other Decks

The **Mythic Tarot deck** shows Justice as Athena, the goddess who was a model for justice in ancient Greece. Lurking in this card is the story of the cursed House of Atreus in Greek mythology. Atreus, the king of Mycenae, broke a promise to Artemis, goddess of hunting, when he did not sacrifice his best sheep in her name. She cursed his family, leading to the murder of the whole family of Agamemnon, Atreus' son, by their own relatives.

The **Medieval Scapini Tarot deck** shows a woman seated between two pillars and two suns, symbolizing clarity of vision. The side panel of four seasons indicates the need for balance.

Prayer

Oh Lord, I know that I could never withstand Thy Justice. I crave for Thy mercy. Show me Thy kindness for you know that to be human is to be weak. Let Thy strength flow to me. Let me distinguish right from wrong and give me the courage to make the right judgement. Let me not be so selfish that I am blind to the needs of others and let me do unto them as I want them to do unto me. Teach me to be fair and see through the pretences of the self. Allow me to rise above difficult situations and evaluate them—not by self-interest but based on morality and honour. Help me to be fearless and face the many weaknesses that reside within me. Let me make the right choices and encourage me to bear the brunt of the consequences without complaining. Let me understand integrity, value and goodness. Let me walk the path of balance so that I finally get united with Thee and gain the kingdom of heaven.

XII
The Hanged Man

XII. The Hanged Man

Voice

'It is all in your mind,' I say. Change your perspective and you might see a different reality. We are too involved in our egos and ourselves and we never see another point of view. Surrender to the divine and give up all your distractions and you will feel as comfortable as I am, suspended between heaven and earth. Accept that God knows better and if He has kept you suspended, there is a good reason for it. Trust God and He will take care of you. Wait, pause, be patient and do not be in a hurry to act. Let higher wisdom operate in your life to give you the insight that you lack. I encourage you to see situations from a different point of view. There is more to life than you understand. Look for something different and this will bring you light. It may initially cause you to feel like your world has been inverted but after a while you will enjoy the position. A new sense of truth will be revealed to you. If you have to sacrifice something for this revelation, is it not worth it? To be able to dislocate yourself from the ego and to connect with the higher self is the aim of all existence and that is what I offer you.

Description

The gallows from which The Hanged Man is suspended forms a cross. There is a halo around the head showing his blessed state. The face bears an expression of deep entrancement, not suffering. He is hung from a living tree, not dead wood. The feet in the air indicate that he is rooted in the universe rather than in the earth and that his centre has shifted from the individual self to the cosmic self. In Jungian terms, The Hanged Man is experiencing the collective consciousness. His hands are unseen as he has handed himself over to the higher powers. In some cards, his hands are shown bound, indicating surrender and in others, they dangle freely. Sometimes, coins fall out of his pockets or hands.

His jacket is blue, the colour of infinity and spirituality, and the hose and the belt are red, the colour of passion and endurance. His shoes are golden as is the rope, indicating high ideals. His jacket is divided into two parts; the lower part has crescents on it, recalling The High Priestess and her neutrality and receptivity. These give us the clue to the inner state of The Hanged Man's mind. One leg is tied to a post and yet he is content with this limitation, suggesting acceptance of the constraints of daily life through good karma, which vindicates existence. The legs of The Hanged Man also form a number four, the number of order and stability, or a swastika, a holy Hindu symbol of the evolution of the universe. He is connected with Christ and is willingly and lovingly submitting himself to his Father's will. It is through his sacrifice that he will gain the kingdom of heaven. While his legs are bent to form a cross, his arms form inverted triangles. This is an alchemical symbol, which signifies the overcoming of the personality and transmutation of the lower passions into pure spiritual gold.

Serenely dangling upside-down, the Hanged Man has relinquished worldly attachments. He has sacrificed a desire for control over his circumstances in order to gain an understanding far greater than his individual self. In letting go, he has gained a new and a profound perspective.

Meaning

The Hanged Man represents sacrifice and resurrection. The image stands for the crucifixion of Christ and the penance of Odin, the Norse god, hanging upside down on Yggdrasil, the Tree of Life (that unites heaven and earth in Norse and pagan mythology) to attain secret knowledge and to unravel the mystery of the universe. It is a highly spiritual card suggesting total surrender to the higher powers, which leads to transformation of the self. The suspended figure indicates that it is important that we halt our worldly activity for inner regeneration and inspiration. For spiritual growth, it is necessary that we become a mere witness to our lives, like the sphinx on the top of The Wheel of Fortune, who watches life unfolding or what is called *sakshi bhav* in Sanskrit.

He is closely associated through the cross-sums with The Empress, which in many mythologies is his mother or wife. He dies and is reborn every year, bringing hope and the promise of resurrection to the world. He is willing to be sacrificed. Number XII is representative of the twelve signs of the zodiac and The Hanged Man is a hero who is representative of the sun going through each sign annually. He is also associated with the Knights of the Minor Arcana who are heroes willing to die for their mission.

The Hanged Man is a card of veiled significance. Its symbolism also points to Egyptian mythology, to the death of Osiris, the god of the after-life, signifying the destruction of the self to bring life to humanity. It usually involves sacrifice of the personal, which becomes sacred as it is brings about a greater good. The figure suggests the reversal of the mind rather than of the body. A reversal of perspective and the way of life, tolerance and understanding as well as patience and faith is the aim of a spiritual seeker.

The Hanged Man is one of the most mysterious cards in the Tarot deck. It is simple, but complex. It attracts, but also disturbs. The Hanged Man is unsettling because it symbolizes the paradox of our lives. The main lesson of The Hanged Man is that we control by letting go and that we win by surrendering. The figure on card XII has made the ultimate surrender—to die on the cross—yet he shines with the glory of divine understanding. He has sacrificed himself, but he emerges the victor. The Hanged Man also tells us that we can move forward by standing still. By suspending time, we can have all the time in the world.

Correspondences

The Hanged Man is associated with the colour blue and the gemstone aquamarine. The associated herb is Irish moss or kelp. The card is linked with the planet Neptune, the planet of purification, martyrdom, self-sacrifice and idealism. The rune representing The Hanged Man is Perth, the rune of chance and mystery or Nied, the rune of necessity.

The Awakening

Surrender and give yourself up to divine influences. Accept the tribulations that come and do not fight against any outcome. Listen to your higher mind and let go. God will take care of you.

The Shadow Aspect

The idea that you are powerful could take a blow. Your ego and arrogance are questioned. What are you resisting? What are you demanding from the universe?

Other Decks

The **Renaissance deck** refers to the myth of Prometheus, the Greek Titan, who suffered intense torture for stealing the fire of the gods—he had defied Zeus to bring fire to human beings. It shows the hanging man beneath a small figure of Prometheus.

In the **Wirth deck**, coins fall from the Hanged Man's pocket, indicating that he has abandoned worldly riches. There are twelve stubs on the two supporting trees, symbolizing the twelve signs of the zodiac, and the hanged man is the solar hero renewing himself every year.

Prayer

Oh Father, You have died on the cross for me. You suffered so that I may have an easier access to heaven. Teach me sacrifice so that I, too, may do something for my brethren. Let me have faith in Thee and not be afraid of the cross that I bear. Let me suffer gladly all the miseries of this world in Thy name and yet be firm in my belief in Thee. Let me surrender my body and soul to Thee and be secure that you will take care of me. Let me see the world with a new perspective that is based on goodness and love, not self-interest. Let me live by Thy creed and depend on Thee rather than on the world. Let my faith be so strong that I can let go in the face of all adversity and accept Thy will. Let me bow my head in Thy service and live in Thy name till the last day of my life.

XIII
Death

XIII. Death

Voice

I ride forth on my white steed and the world bows down to me. No one can challenge me for I am death—the only reality of existence. All that are born will die. People are scared of me but if I were not there, there would only be the old, the stagnant and the boring. Without new beginnings or new life, new ideas or new opportunities, you would get choked. I bring death-like changes in your life that open up new vistas after destroying the old. Change is another essential thing that I aid. I encourage transformation and renewal. Unless the old leaves are shed, how can the new ones sprout? Welcome me with open arms, for I signal the end of outmoded ways of life. I blow away all the cobwebs and give you an opportunity to begin life anew. I end the status quo and generate new thought patterns and new ways. I promise rebirth after disintegration. I bring you a new dawn with exciting potential ... only if you give up what you are clinging to. Let go and accept the storms of change that are brewing in your life. Go with the upheavals and accept me as the ultimate release.

Description

The mysterious horseman is a golden skeleton. He rides a well-bridled horse, and moves slowly across the field. The golden colour of the skeleton is the colour of spiritual progress. The skeleton is the toughest part of the human body and survives long after the flesh is gone. Death bears a black banner signifying chaos before it takes shape. It is emblazoned with the mystic rose, which stands for life, beauty, rebirth and immortality. It is the same white rose that we have seen in the hands of the Fool. The armour Death is wearing shows him to be invincible and unconquerable. No one can triumph over him. Death rides a white horse, white being the colour of purity. He is the ultimate purifier. All beings are reborn fresh, new and pure. The river behind him is the Styx that transports dead souls, while the lake above it is the lake of unconsciousness or the ultimate source into which everything flows.

All are powerless before the rider. A king, child and maiden fall prostrate before him, while a priest awaits his arrival with clasped hands. All the figures on the card are aspects of the self: the child is innocence, the king is worldly power, the maiden is purity and sorrow and the priest is our spiritual beliefs and faith. Death is a great equalizer; everyone is the same to him. All are subjected by Death to the universal and natural laws. It puts an end to illusions and dualities. In the end, all are one and all go back to one source. The Hindu concept *aham brahamasmi* (I am Brahma or the source) is illustrated by this card.

The sun and the moon are implicit in this card; the towers seen in The Moon card frame a rising sun here. Night and day are depicted in this card, reinforcing the deliberate, strong contrast—light and dark or black and white.

Meaning

The sun shining on the edge of the horizon reminds us of the new day and new opportunities. The sun symbolizes immortality—it appears to die every night, but is reborn fresh and new every morning, signifying that Death is really just a change. The two towers guard the gateway to the sun, symbolizing the ego that needs to be crossed and the knowledge that is needed to gain immortality. We keep coming back to this plane until we learn our lessons and it is only when we learn them that we merge with the source.

The background of the card is a neutral grey, showing Death's impartiality. This archetype teaches you to let go of outworn and outgrown ways of life and move forward. Death is a clearing away of the old to make way for the new. The card of Death continues the work of the earlier card, The Hanged Man, where surrender will lead to total change. It is a precursor to resurrection. The card represents the death of the old self—although not necessarily physical death. It indicates the death of the ego as the only way of moving ahead. It is in the card of Death that we see our deepest fears reflected. We think that dying means annihilation, but the card shows us that it is not an end, but a transition into a new state. Death happens continually, at many levels—each moment is the end of the previous moment and the beginning of the next; we die in the present so that the future can unfold. Death often represents an important ending that will initiate a great change. It signals the end of a cycle, a moment when a door is closing. At such times, there will be sadness and reluctance to let go—it is important to acknowledge the loss—but also relief and a sense of completion. Death and time are closely linked. Both are often shown carrying a scythe, and both are often called the Reaper, the one who takes in the harvest.

The card suggests transformation. Symbolically, the card represents the cycles of nature and constant change in our own development as we move towards the final merging. The time of harvest marks the end of a cycle in which the seeds of a new season are sown. As the earth undergoes a yearly cycle of death and renewal, we too, undergo many such cycles. If we resist change we experience pain, but if we have faith and accept change we will emerge like the legendary phoenix, rising from the ashes and soaring upward.

Death is associated through its cross-sum with Key IV, The Emperor. The Emperor takes power through death, wields the power of death and is brought to power through death. In addition to The Emperor, Death is associated with the Queens, the thirteenth card of each suit of the Minor Arcana. The card of Death is also associated with the Hindu god Shiva, referred to as the destroyer, who has the power to annihilate.

Correspondence

The colour associated with Death is blue-green, the herb is the elderflower and the gemstone is black tournamaline. The rune connected with the card of Death is Eihwaz—it takes its name from the yew tree, which symbolizes death. Death is associated with the sun sign Scorpio—represented by three creatures: the scorpion, the grey lizard and eagle—which governs the organs of reproduction and elimination. The Death card indicates the evolution from the lower to the higher aspects of the psyche.

The Awakening

Profound change is the beginning of a new life—welcome it, for it offers liberation and new opportunities. Old patterns will go, which is essential, or rotting and stagnation will persist.

The Shadow Aspect

There is a resistance to change, leading to stagnation and a tendency to inertia. The upheavals that come will be the result of your blindness.

Other Decks

In **Mythic Tarot**, the image on the card of Death is Hades, king of the underworld. In Greek mythology, after the overthrow of Kronos, the leader of the Titans, his sons—Zeus, Poseidon, the god of the sea and Hades, the god of death—divided his kingdom into the three realms of the sky, ocean and the underworld. The kingdom of Hades was the underworld, which he ruled with great power for his laws were irrevocable. The image of Death is also shown with a scythe in many Tarot decks where the reference is to Saturn, the god of time. Time is referred to as mortality, while death is called the Reaper.

In the **Visconti deck**, the skeleton is shown with remnants of a shroud tied round the head and he stands on the edge of a precipice.

Prayer

I die a thousand deaths every day and yet I am afraid of dying. I resist change and fear losing everything. Oh Father, I know that death is but a change yet why can't I see it like that? Why don't I have enough faith in Thee to look death in the eye? Why do I tremble at a mere whisper of death around me? Let me surrender to Thy will. Show me the way that leads me to Thee, away from these fears and traumas. I know that whoever is born will die and yet I do not have the strength or courage to face the ultimate reality of my existence. Open my eyes and let me accept the truth. Be by my side when my time comes so that I am able to move into Thy presence without any pain and fear. Hold my hand, my Lord, and guide me through all the turbulence of my life … let me merge with Thee forever.

XIV
Temperance

XIV. Temperance

Voice

I bring harmony to your life by teaching you how to mix and mingle different things to create something beautiful. Harmony is about the right proportion and right combination. I can heal all your pain. I can create gold with my blending and mix the perfect elixir for happiness. There are always two sides, two aspects and two perspectives—look at these carefully and you will be able to integrate the apparent opposites to form a new whole that is perfect. Find solutions not problems, find peace not war, find love and joy not bitterness and resentment. Look at me and learn to find your balance between the two worlds, between the conscious and the subconscious, and use both to bring joy to your existence. It is not difficult to flow like the water that is in my chalice. Seek my guidance to create a unified self and to adapt to changing circumstances of life. Come to me to heal your wounds, to soothe your life and find peace in your soul.

Description

The angel shown in the card is Archangel Michael robed in white, a symbol of purity. His red wings are a symbol of desire. This indicates the essence of the card—the harmony and balance of desire and purity. The opposing forces can be combined to create perfection and peace. He stands with one foot on the earth and the other in water, indicating that the material world needs to be balanced with the spiritual world. He pours the water of life from the silver cup of the intuitive unconsciousness in his left hand into the golden cup of the rational consciousness and then back again. This depicts the entry of the spirit into matter and the influence of matter on the spirit. The process of mixing continues till a perfect wholeness is achieved. There is no spillage, indicating that discipline and self-control are required to live a happy life. The golden path near the angel leads to the mountains of wisdom and self-knowledge. Irises, symbols of thought, bloom besides him. Signifying the illumination of the spirit, these flowers are sacred to Iris, the Greek goddess of the rainbow. The angel wears a solar star on his brow, indicating the purification that is going on and showing that he is related to the sun. He has a seven-pointed star over his heart, which stands for the seven *chakras*. On his breast is a square with a triangle within it, which is the symbol of the sacred book of Tarot, indicating the secret wisdom that is revealed through the esoteric sciences.

Meaning

The word 'temperance' is from 'temper', which is a firing process in alchemy that transforms base metal into gold—thus the guidance of the angel through esoteric alchemy transforms an ordinary person to an enlightened soul. For this, mixing and remixing is required till the right combination is achieved. The unconscious and the conscious need to blend perfectly in the silver and the gold chalices and refine the opposing elements within a human personality. It is like the great churning of the ocean in Indian mythology, which resulted in the emergence of nectar or *amrit*.

The elixir mixed by the angel is the secret potion which is the solution to all human ills. When a human being gains the understanding of the beauty and power of his soul, he too, can create such an elixir.

Temperance is a card of vibrant energy. It indicates that no experience is useless and should be used to improve the future. The constant movement of the mind can lead to great ideas and knowledge. Temperance, like the Justice card, indicates the need for balance and tranquillity at a higher plane. This, along with strength, justice and prudence, form the cardinal virtues of the medieval world.

The stance of the angel represents the need to 'test the waters' before jumping headlong into unknown circumstances. In most modern Tarot decks, Temperance stands between Death and The Devil. The card gives the hope that all is not dark after Death and prepares you for The Devil and The Tower. This is a card of respite, of rest, before the Fool moves to his toughest lessons in the next two cards.

Temperance is associated through its cross-sum with the Hierophant, who brings the lessons of the other world into this world. Temperance demonstrates the wisdom of both the worlds and shows how to use it for fulfillment in this life. It is the card of good health in all areas—physical, mental and emotional. When illness or disease is a concern, Temperance holds the promise of vitality and well-being.

For the ancient Greeks, Temperance was the central virtue of civic life. It represented the restraint of appetite, whether for food, drink, or sex. In classical philosophy, therefore, it stands for the subordination of the physical desires to higher, rational ideals. Nothing is forbidden, so long as there is no excess. All aspects of life should be harmonious. According to the Bible, Archangel Michael rid the heaven of the dragon/Satan and his demons and he can slay the dragon within each of us. His role is the same in the card of Temperance.

Correspondence

The colour of the card is blue, the herb is *Echinacea* and the gemstones are rosequartz and aquamarine. The rune associated with this card is Ingwaz, which signifies energy and action. The angel can be seen as a hermaphrodite, the child of Hermes, the messenger of the Greek gods, and Aphrodite, the Greek goddess of love, showing a balance between the sexes. The astrological sign closest to it is Sagittarius, the teacher of truth, enthusiasm, tolerance and beauty.

The Awakening

Moderation and tempering, coordination and healing are experienced. Follow the natural laws and you will evolve. Find the right combination for your soul by remixing and balancing aspects of your being.

The Shadow Aspect

Extreme actions and reactions will get a negative response from the universe. The shadow aspect indicates unfortunate relationships or situations that do not work well, quarrels and competition, rather than living in harmony.

Other Decks

In the **Medieval Scapini deck,** the water-bearing angel holds chalices in the shape of the crescent moon and is accompanied by a lion, indicating the opposites of feminine and the masculine energies. The alchemical process is central to the card.

In the **Renaissance deck,** the images look like the image of the sun sign Aquarius, the water-bearer sign, with the image of the angel pouring water from one cup to another.

Prayer

Oh Lord, teaches me moderation and balance so that I can walk the middle path denoted by you. Let me reconcile the opposite elements of my life in a harmonious whole. Blend all ingredients in me till I get the right combination of tranquillity and peace. Purify my action and thoughts and show me the right path that will lead me to the lofty heights of spiritual progress. Let Thy alchemy transform me from a base metal to pure gold. Teach me how to mix the elements of my life to create the perfect elixir that will be a solution to all my ills. Bring me peace and goodness, stillness and richness of my soul. Take my pain away, and let me find bliss.

XV
The Devil

XV. The Devil

Voice

I am the creature of the dark and I will show you all that you want to hide. I do not know anything except sensations and that is what I use to mislead gullible creatures. Come to me and I will light the torch of lust in you. I sit on a half-cube of knowledge but I know your weakness. If you want to lie, cheat, be deceitful and destructive, I know exactly what you should do. I lose power if you face me and accept your weaknesses for I revel in making you fearful and worried. It is when you are weak that I am strong. My chains are meant to bind you to me but the wise know that the chains are loose and they can slip out of them if they want to. I can do nothing if you don't allow me to and I wilt if you look me in the eye. My approach is to keep you confused. I have all kinds of temptations to distract you from your real purpose of life and keep you busy in temporal pleasure. Beware, as I want nothing less than your soul.

Description

The monstrous red-eyed, horned, winged and clawed Devil is perched on a half-cube, signifying that he only has half-knowledge, which is of the sensory side of experience. His horns and face are that of a goat and his ears are of a donkey, representing the obstinacy and stubbornness of the material world. His bat-like wings associate him with the creatures of the night that cannot see in the light and with witchcraft. His right arm is raised in curses as opposed to the Hierophant whose hand is raised in blessing. The inverted five-pointed star on his forehead indicates evil intent, destructive tendencies, negativity and the need to manipulate others. The eyes of The Devil are glazed with sensory pleasures, showing a drunken stupor and obsessive lust that lack any understanding.

Chained to the half-cube are two nude figures, Adam and Eve. The figures are chained by their own wrong choices. Their chains are loose and can be removed if they want to be free. They are dominated by their bestial selves, as shown by their horns and hoofs. The Tree of Knowledge and the Tree of Life appear in distorted form. With his left hand, The Devil lights the fire of lust in the man's tail, while the woman's tail ends in a bunch of grapes, which suggests a state of intoxication and loss of control of the senses. This card is the bestialized version of Key VI—The Lovers.

Meaning

The Devil embodies the negative aspects that civilization has taught us to despise, the shadowy side of our personality that carries our fear and self-loathing. Like the figures chained in the card, our weaknesses hold us captive through fear and disgust. The Devil represents the side of us that is not known or understood consciously, which frightens us. It relates to black magic, discontent, depression and illness. It is the bondage to the material and represents force that is wrongly used.

We all carry our devils within us—our fears, past traumas and dark desires. We cannot find freedom from these until we look at them honestly and understand them. We will have to face the devil within us, for it is only then that he will hold no terror for us and we can walk away from darkness. Key XV depicts our weakness, but also the solution. Seeing and accepting the dark side, means freedom from it.

Three Tarot suits appear prominently in this card. The Devil's wings represent air, the suit of Swords. The torch in his hands and the flames in the tail of the male represent fire, the suit of Wands. The grapes in the tail of the female invoke earth, the suit of Pentacles. Only water or Cups are overtly missing. The Devil is the creature of the subconscious mind—he is found in all areas of life and we need to be alert to avoid him.

The Devil card has several meanings. It can represent vices and addictions and is about temptation, seduction and sex—all our primitive needs that have to be understood, but not allowed to rule our lives. This card explores materialism and excessive attachment to valuables, food or drugs, lack of control, obsession, raw ambition, lies and deceit.

Among all the cards, The Devil stands out as interestingly different, because no other card is so one-sided. Most cards urge balance, unity and restraint, but this card revels in extremity. Where the occult is concerned, this is the most powerful and dangerous card in the deck, with a powerful significance of a negative kind. In Jungian terms, The Devil is the dark side of ourselves that we repress. It represents aspects of the self that are not acknowledged or mentioned, which is why he holds such a terror for us. Despite its fearsome appearance, this card stands for weakness, for The Devil can hold sway only when we are weak. It always has negative connotations when it occurs in a reading.

The Devil represents the ego that blinds us to our faults and is the false importance given to the self that disconnects a person from the reality of existence. The Devil means lack of hope and faith, when the world is seen as black with no hope or possibilities. These are the shackles that keep you tied to The Devil with no desire or strength to free your soul from his clutches.

Another view is that The Devil is not really Satan at all, but Pan, the half-goat Greek god of nature or Dionysius, the Greek god of wine. They are gods of pleasure and abandon, of wild behaviour and unbridled desires.

Correspondences

The Devil is associated with the colour black, the gemstone black onyx and the herb, lobella. The Devil is associated with earth and the sun sign of Capricorn. The rune is Nauthiz, associated with the dark, repressed side of a person.

The Awakening

Bondage to negativity is because of a lack of understanding of true human nature. You are a spirit and have the power to free yourself from all chains. Realize your essence and go beyond all limitations. Recognize The Devil within you and confront it. That is your liberation.

The Shadow Aspect

The waning influence of The Devil shows that there is some light at the end of the tunnel, indicating the beginning of spiritual understanding and the overcoming of negativity and bondage.

Other Decks

The **Renaissance deck** shows Pan as the Devil. Pan was so ugly that his own mother ran away from him in horror. He is the untamed god of nature and sexuality.

The **Visconti deck** shows The Devil with female breasts, with the legs of a goat and the ears of an ass to emphasize his lust and excessive sexuality.

Prayer

Oh Lord, forgive me for I am weak and tainted. The mask of goodness that I wear is only for the outer world. Deep down I am filled with desires of the flesh, of greed, of deceit, of fears of the unknown within me. I am blind to the needs of others as my own needs are so paramount. Oh Father, heal me, make me see the world as it is and not through my ego. Break the chains of my ignorance so that I can see the truth. Let me understand my senses and not get completely overpowered by the pleasure that they offer. Oh Lord, be by my side and teach me humility, simplicity and kindness. Make me positive and honest. Give me the courage to look my devil in the eye and be free of him forever.

XVI
The Tower

XVI. The Tower

Voice

I am the awakener. I come to shake you out of your complacency and to make you think about your values, beliefs and choices. I come to disrupt your preconceived ideas and notions about yourself and your life. The structure of your ego that you have so lovingly built will come crashing down in my presence. For I bring to you the karmic lessons that you need to learn. If you thought that you were unreachable, think again. All those who have been elevated have to come down to know what the reality of existence is and to be refined and purified. I break down all your boundaries and destroy your safety net so that you can give up the obsolete way of life you are clinging to. You will never experience a flash of insight as bright as when my lightning strikes you. My lightning is the divine fire that will destroy all that is dross so that you may create something exciting and beautiful with a new understanding of your true self. You could find it painful but you need to learn those lessons or you will be lost. The divine grace will be with you even when you fall and you will be held safely before you reach the ground.

Description

The Tower is a dramatic image of a carefully constructed structure that is shattered by the enormous power and violence of nature. The stone tower is standing alone on a foundation that is weak—this indicates that any edifice built on a wrong premise, to perpetuate the ego, is bound to collapse. The black background signifies the darkness of the soul. The clouds are grey, representing misfortune and turbulence. The lightning in the card is the same flash that lights up the lantern of The Hermit—the purifying energy that burns all dross. The lightning, shaped like the arrow, strikes the top of the tower, or the crown of materialistic thought. It has three flaming windows. There are two figures in the card that have either jumped from the windows or have fallen down; both their expressions show shock. They correspond to the chained prisoners in The Devil card. The figures, representing the dual nature of man, are clothed in red and blue to show a mixture of self-conscious (planned) and subconscious (unplanned) activities. The woman is crowned with false knowledge and subconscious motives. No one is spared from the consequences of their actions—even the crowned beings are not exempt from the result of their karmas.

Falling with the figures are twenty-two Yods, which represent God's grace or the life force. This indicates that even in the worst moment of punishment, the grace of God is always with you and will save you. The twenty-two Yods are also representative of the twenty-two cards of the Major Arcana.

The Tower is the only man-made structure in the Major Arcana. It is the edifice that we build around our weaknesses as our defence, to hide the true self from the world and even from our own selves. It is also the facade that we present to the world.

The lightning bolt breaks down existing life patterns that you are familiar with in order to make you realize that you had built your tower of self-protection on the sands of false ideas that are bound to give way. The lightning flash symbolizes a sudden, momentary glimpse of truth which jolts you into facing your inadequacies. The Tower leaves a person humbled. After the experience of The Tower, the self will be open to reconstructing a more realistic self-image. It brings you face to face with your ego and forces you to question your belief systems and sense of security. It shakes the very foundations of your being and the way you operate in the world. The cards of Death and The Devil deal with personal issues, indicating that the confrontation is with the inner world. With The Tower, it is your relationship with the world that is challenged and your external life comes under scrutiny. The ego is exposed and then struck. The Tower card strips down all pretences to expose shortcomings, sometimes causing a public catharsis, when matters come out in the open. The Tower usually signifies a major negative change that has occurred or will happen in your life.

Meaning

The Tower follows the card of The Devil and represents breaking his bonds. The Tower can be seen as a place of imprisonment and illusion and the destruction of this edifice paves the way to an experience of freedom in our lives. The Tower also shows the illusion of considering ourselves 'above' others. When The Tower of deception, ego and illusion is destroyed, we are able to face the truth and reality without the trappings of false beliefs.

The Tower is the turning point for The Fool. He can either go back to The Devil by turning away from his true self and the lessons of The Tower or move ahead in humility and wisdom to reach the insight of The Star. Only if he accepts and sees his limitations, however painful, he can move ahead.

The Tower is ruled by Mars and is about destruction and the immediacy of change. It can have a disorienting effect because it is never pleasant or easy to pull down all that is false in your life. Whenever this card shows up, a pertinent question to ask yourself is, 'What structures in my life are breaking down?'. It is a wake-up call from the universe to jolt you back to reality.

There is a lot of movement in the card. The clouds are whirling, fires are burning, the crown is toppling and the figures are falling. Everything is moving at high speed, except The Tower. It is our frozen sense of self that refuses to see what is happening around us.

In our Tarot journey, we try to retain our sense of self. This starts with The Magician and piece by piece, we build our ego, which is represented by The Tower. A sudden occurrence like the lightning in the card can suddenly strike and the whole structure that we have built comes crashing down.

Correspondence

The related colour is scarlet red, the gemstone is garnet and the herb is garlic. The rune associated with The Tower is Hagalaz, which shows us that a radical change will come.

The Awakening

It is time to examine the ego and let go of preoccupations with the self. All that is wrong and irrelevant needs to go from your life. Realize your essence and go beyond your limitations. The ego centres will be struck by some force and in the flash you will see the true path. Pain is inevitable for no growth is possible without pain.

The Shadow Aspect

The time to expel the ego has come. Freedom always comes at a cost, which means that a feeling of oppression and false accusations may need to be dealt with. The Devil is within you, not in the extraneous world.

Other Decks

In the **Scapini deck,** The Tower represents the seven-storeyed Tower of Babel built on sand; each storey stands for one of the seven deadly sins: pride, greed, envy, anger, lust, gluttony and sloth.

In the **Renaissance deck,** tiny images of Phaeton (who tried to drive his father's sun chariot but was killed by Zeus when he failed to control it and almost set the earth on fire) and Icarus (who plummeted to his death when he tried to fly with wings made of feathers and wax) are added in the corner of the Tower of Babel and represent arrogance because both were rash.

In the **Wirth deck,** the crown has the colours of the four elements and the lightning represents the divine fire essential for alchemical change to take place.

Prayer

Oh Lord, I have lost the sight of my goals and myself. I am in a labyrinth and am unable to find the way out. Oh Father, break down this tower of ignorance and arrogance so that I can find Thy light. I am in the darkness of selfishness and isolated from the rest of the world in thought and feeling—let me reconnect with them in humility and simplicity. Let me realize that I am but a frail human being and it has been your blessings that have given me power. Let me see my false pride and false sense of self-importance and know how far that has brought me from Thee. Oh Father, help me to find the right way and come home to Thee in a new tomorrow and rebuild my life based on righteous thinking and values.

XVII
The Star

XVII. The Star

Voice

There is beauty in your life if you will just see it. The stars are shining but you need to open your eyes to experience their light. Life is not just pain and unhappiness. I come to show you the other side. I am the insight that you need to make life happy and full of love. Look beneath the surface, see the harmony beneath appearances and your world will change. Use your senses to connect with your being. I herald that beauty which you crave, the hope that you seek and the benediction that you need. There is true love that can be given and received. Open yourself and you will receive it. My path leads you to meditation and beyond. Know me and you will know yourself and see the world in the right light. Awaken your chakras. *My waters purify and cleanse you of all past pain and the memory of it. I have nothing to hide for I want nothing from you. I want to give, and in giving there is great pleasure.*

Description

A naked woman kneels by the water, with one foot in the water of a pool and the other foot on land. Her stance is one of prayer. Above her head, the stars are shining. In each hand she holds a jug. She pours the water from one jug into the pool of the unconscious. From the other jug she pours water on the land in five streams, which represent the five senses. The pouring is a part of a cleansing process; the water is healing. She knows that the senses need to be nourished in the right way for inner growth. Pouring water in the pool of the unconscious signifies meditation and alignment with the universal energies—healing both the conscious and the subconscious mind is the final liberation. The bird nesting on the tree is the soul and bears a resemblance to the ibis, a bird venerated by the ancient Egyptians as a symbol of Thoth, the Egyptian god of wisdom. The sky is clear blue and suggests inspiration, creativity and peace. The lush green surroundings indicate abundance and healing. Her tranquillity comes from the insight she has gained. She is the calm after the storm and suggests that resolution is at hand.

The same maiden in the card of Temperance was carefully balancing her emotions. The emotional waters are now emptied and she has let go of her emotions as the time for restriction is over. Her nakedness is a symbol of her acceptance, her rejection of pretences and of her acceptance of herself as she truly is without any artifice. She has nothing to hide or fear for she has been stripped of illusion in the previous card of The Tower.

The pitchers contain the nectar of life, the healing waters that can purify and change. All the four elements are represented in this card—the water element is the pool and the pitcher filled with water suggests fluidity, movement and emotions. The earth is represented by the trees and the flowers, suggesting security and safety. Air is represented by the bird, which implies the soul flying to meet the divine; the fire element is represented by the bright stars that shine with an inner fire, bringing optimism and hope. The sky suggests the infinite expanse of the mind.

Meaning

The star is a symbol of guidance, representing the Star of Bethlehem, which led the three wise men to Baby Jesus. The maiden symbolizes guidance, intuition and higher consciousness, which are our ultimate guides. The big star symbolizes the ending of the karmic debt that binds us to this life. The seven stars are the seven planets: the sun, the moon, Mercury, Venus, Mars, Jupiter and Saturn, each defining the character. They are also the seven *chakras*, which are energy nodes in the human body directly connected with healing (in Indian spirituality). Their activation leads to perfect spiritual, mental, emotional and physical health. The eight-pointed stars are the symbols of Venus, and reinforce the love, peace and hope offered by the card.

The card does not suggest immediate results, but indicates unexpected aid. It is a card that assures you, consoles you and gives you the encouragement that you need. It indicates that liberation is just around the corner, and supports you in every possible way to allow you to move ahead to a glorious future. The Star expands your radiance and puts you in touch with the beauty of your soul. This connection brings peace, hope and deep insight into yourself. It represents the end of a period of change and turmoil.

True love and true friendship are governed by The Star. It signifies the bonding of souls and relationships that are based on inner connections and mutual love. This card augurs all the good things in life—the dark clouds have passed and positive energy flows back into life. Fortune smiles with the promise of fulfillment. The card make you feel blessed and protected.

The Star brings you the gift of intuition and healing. It reveals a loving phase with renewed understanding. Your ability to let go of damaging memories has been strengthened by contact with your true self. Now you are able to forgive and forget. The card can also indicate that you might become the centre of attention and perhaps, even the star of the show. Wisdom, spiritual enlightenment and progress toward your goal is indicated by the Star.

Correspondences

The Star is associated with the sun sign of Aquarius and the rune is Dagaz, which indicates the balance of opposites. The colours are pale yellow, blue and violet, the herb is star anise or skullcap and the gemstones are turquoise and aquamarine. Like Aquarius, it is focused on the future.

The Awakening

A time to heal and be at peace has come. The storms are gone and the dawn brings hope and love. The card indicates spiritual progress and deep insight into the inner self. Generousity renews the soul.

The Shadow Aspect

Perhaps there is too much dwelling on negative thoughts. There is a lack of spiritual strength to forge ahead and overcome problems. The shadow aspect suggests lack of hope and optimism, lack of insight and understanding and chances of physical or mental illness. Doubt and stubbornness dominate. A loss of friendship or love is indicated.

Other Decks

The **Wirth deck** shows a young girl pouring water into the pool of memory, which lies at the edge of the underworld. Those returning from the land of the dead would drink from this pool and forget their mystical experiences.

Prayer

I thank Thee for the wonderful gift of all the senses that give me so much pleasure. Let me use them in your service. Let me discover the stars in my life. Let me reach them in your name. Let me awaken the divine energy within me so that I access all your blessings. Let me know Thy love and let my heart connect with Thee. Let me live in the reflected glory and create the same love all around me. Give me hope in my darkest hour and the balm of true love in my pain. Let me see beneath the world of appearances to gain insight and to have faith in your plan for me. Inspire me to be unselfish and give with all my heart to others as you give to me.

XVIII
The Moon

XVIII. The Moon

Voice

I am the power of the subconscious mind. I manifest in dreams and intuitive impulses that you do not understand. I am the ebb and flow of time and I bring constant change. Be like the ocean that flows with my phases, dance to my universal rhythm and you will conquer all doubts. Learn from me about things that are hidden and arcane, break through the illusions and primordial fears. Let go of your memories for they exist only in your mind. I am the reflected glory of the sun but have developed my own powers and so can you, for you too are the reflected glory of the Lord. My gentle and cool energy can provide love and healing but you will need to trust yourself and have faith in my powers. I can bring you aching beauty and poetry of the soul—revel in these but don't try to hold on to them for they are as changeable as my phases. Break down the towers of your ego and surrender to life. Grow toward the divine and I will show you the way in the night. Trust your instincts and flow with me.

Description

The card shows a dark, undulating landscape illuminated only by the moonlight—the light is a reflection and hence an illusion. Each of us must go through the difficult journey of The Moon to reach the sun on the other side. There are perils in this landscape and yet it is also a scene of great power and beauty. There is much to be learned in this card if one can understand and cope with the contradictions here. In the foreground of The Moon card you will see a crab emerging from a pool of water. The crab represents us. Like the crab, we have a hard ego shell that we erect to protect the self. This needs to break for only when the ego dissolves is reality visible to us. It is painful but it is an experience that we all have to go through. The pool is the collective subconscious from which all creation emerges. Beyond the water is the path that we need to follow. There are distractions and fears that have to be faced. There are obscure patches of night—eerie landscapes, snarling wolves, winding paths and the lure of empty promises. There are two towers, one of which is already damaged. These dark presences, airless and brooding, need to be negotiated. Apart from being phallic symbols, the towers represent the trappings of this world. These are illusions found along the path of our higher purpose. The towers also remind us that if we build our lives upon false illusions, all our hopes and endeavours will inevitably come crashing down. These represent the false ego. Beyond The Moon is the sun, and a promise of hope. The dog and the wolf are aspects of the mind, the domesticated and disciplined aspects that can help us on this journey or the wild and the primordial instincts that need to be understood to prevent them from harming us. The Yods are with us to help us cross this morbid landscape.

Meaning

The card represents the landscape of the mind and imagination. The dog and the wolf are creatures of the mind, one tame and the other wild. Both need to be handled. The primordial creature arises from the darker hidden facets of the human mind; it represents the instincts that cannot be denied. The calm face of The Moon is the intuition that shows the way and the dew of divine help is always there to help us.

The Moon is all about vision and illusion, madness, genius and poetry. It can be a frightening card in that it warns of hidden enemies, tricks and falsehood in our lives. But it should also be remembered that this is a card of great creativity, of powerful magic, primal feelings and intuition. Trust your intuition and move on confidently.

This card has to do with both dreams and nightmares. It may indicate a particularly difficult emotional time. Instead of connecting with the negative aspects of The Moon card, focus on creativity and intuition as an expression of The Moon. This can put you in touch with deep understanding, visions and insight.

No one is immune to the influence of the moon. When she is waxing you feel yourself expand and blossom, creativity and poetry awakens in your soul and you become energized. When the moon is waning, you shrink and become unsure of yourself. Fears and morbid imagination grip you and you become a victim of your nightmares. Understand this pull of The Moon and go beyond it—this is the liberation that you will achieve.

This card indicates how the mind confuses and stalls itself. This is the power of The Moon. It manifests itself to impact your mind, but could pull you in different directions, causing havoc and leading to bad decisions and actions. It is only the understanding and awareness of The

Moon's influence that will deliver you from this. The message of the card is to trust your instincts and use them to chart the right course for your life. The solution is to see things objectively. Despite the powerful feelings that The Moon evokes, The Fool must steer his course through troubled waters. Handling the emotions correctly is the issue highlighted by The Moon card.

The Moon is feminine and it is important that both men and women recognize its feminine aspects. When The Moon appears in a Tarot spread, it often represents emotional challenges, inner turmoil and psychic disturbance. There can be a lack of clarity in dealing with the mundane world, or excessive dreaming. Things may not be what they seem. Trickery, deceit and inordinate fear are aspects of The Moon. Knowing this and working through it all is the role that the spiritual warrior must play.

Some people say The Moon is a negative card, full of deceit. Others look at it as an intuitive card that leads to divine grace. The High Priestess is connected with The Moon. However, she is the intuitive and the creative aspect of The Moon—she is still and inward-looking while the card of The Moon has movement and looks towards the sun.

Correspondences

The colour associated with The Moon card is silver, the herb is valerian and the gem is the moonstone. The sun sign is Pisces/Cancer. The rune is Isa, which represents the stillness and purity of ice.

The Awakening

Discriminate between illusion and reality, morbid imagination and spiritual insight. The path may be treacherous and mysterious, but fear is the chief enemy.

The Shadow Aspect

Be practical and real, grounded and centred. Do not get carried away by emotions. No risks should be taken for the danger is that The Moon will create illusions.

Other Decks

The **Renaissance deck** shows a huge moon, under which two maidens play music, which symbolizes the creative potential of the card. In the top right corner is Artemis, the goddess of the moon and hunting, and in the other corner is the hunted stag.

In the **Wirth deck**, the card shows a dark pool of forgetfulness, which lies near the pool of memory in the underworld. It is said that a soul must drink from both the pools before life can be started anew.

Prayer

Oh Lord, let me be as beautiful as the queen of the universe. Let me be inspired with love, music and poetry. I am tired of the changing kaleidoscope of my existence. Please bring stability to my life. Let me be constant in my pursuit of eternal beauty, goodness and happiness. Let me not get diverted by imaginary fears. Let the mist of illusions clear from my mind. Show me the truth so that I may see things as they really are. Teach me to be discerning. Show me the intuitive way out of my difficulties. Stop my cogitation and show me the way of faith. Take away my fear and my morbid imagination that have led me to a dead end. Instead, let Thy grace fall on me to ease my burden. Heal my soul and lead me to the path of deliverance.

XIX
The Sun

XIX. The Sun

Voice

Look within and you will find me at the centre of your being for I am the sun, the source and provider of life. From time immemorial, I have driven the darkness away. I will do the same in your life so give yourself a chance. I am Father Time that resolves and dissolves everything. My brightness dazzles your eyes and makes you understand joy and pleasure. My warmth cocoons you and makes you feel safe and cosy. My light brings a new dawn and new beginnings of hope and peace. Look at me and feel liberated from the shackles of sadness, pain and disillusionment for these can be shed and new shoots of life will emerge once the old and the decayed ones have run their course. Success will come with faith, confidence and hope. You will triumph over your problems. Believe in yourself and in me. Come to me and I will show you how to turn your life around. Feel safe, for you have come home.

Description

An infant with a luminous human face rides a white horse under The Sun. He bears a red standard of victory. The walled garden with all its limitations is behind him for he has come out of it. He is laughing, for there is nothing to fear now. He needs no clothes—there is nothing to hide. He does not have a saddle or a bridle, signifying that he has achieved a perfect balance between the conscious and subconscious mind. He is secure and sure of where he wants to go and he trusts the horse to take him there. There is no control required as there is no conflict between him and the horse. The horse represents power and movement in a new direction. The Sun is a larger than life presence, shining benignly at the top of the card. The rays of The Sun are straight as well as wavy. The straight rays represent the action of the conscious mind while the wavy rays represent the vibration of the subconscious.

The child is also a symbol of a new beginning. Nudity indicates communicating with our true self without fear or shame. The sunflowers indicate hope and the celebration of the truth of existence, their golden colours being symbolic of good fortune and abundance. They turn towards creation, suggesting good fortune for the child and his future.

The four sunflowers represent the four kingdoms of the world—that of animals, minerals, vegetables and human beings. They also represent the four suits of the Minor Arcana and the four elements.

The wall suggests the wall of division that we build around ourselves, which has to dissolve if we are to be liberated. The card suggests a breakthrough and the joys associated with breaking down limitations.

Meaning

The Sun is the symbol of certainty and reliability. No matter how bleak the situation may be, you can always count on the sun to rise every morning. It is an assurance that there is order in a chaotic universe. This is a breakthrough card, which is a clear message that The Sun will shine brightly in your life. A seemingly hopeless situation will change and The Sun card will illuminate the true path and the right solution.

The Sun card implies that it is time to communicate your thoughts and feelings and express your dreams. It is also a card of long-anticipated opportunity. It always indicates success and happiness. The Star gives hope and direction whereas The Sun shows you the path of positive actions to realize your innermost dreams. It is a card of action, showing you that it is time to stop hiding. All wrongs will be righted and brightness, truth and clarity will prevail.

The Sun symbolizes many facets of life, depending on how you look at it. The great ordeal of The Moon has passed, and you have emerged into the light, stronger and wiser. The war of the self has ended and there is peace. This is truly a time to celebrate, of good triumphing over evil.

The warmth of The Sun in this card is not harsh like the strong lightning bolt in the card of The Tower nor is it a subtle glow as seen in the card of The Star. It has moderate warmth and light. This moderation between extremes is the goal of the spiritual traveller. The connotations of the card are success, happiness, love and good health and the blazing vitality that is life-enhancing.

The card of The Sun is associated with the attainment of knowledge. The conscious mind prevails over the fears and illusions of The Moon card and is renewed through the brightness of The Sun card that dispels ignorance. It also indicates artistic and creative talents. If you are dealing with new ideas, concepts, creativity and invention, you will find success. It is a card of intellect, clarity of mind and youthful energy.

The Sun suggests happiness in love, marriage, friendship and life as a whole. It signifies commitment—the child in this card could indicate the possibility of a pregnancy. The Sun indicates the pleasure in daily existence and in the simple things of life, a sense of completion. It also symbolizes universal or unconditional love, the type which can never be destroyed and is not dependent on the other person loving you in return. It is the type of love that a parent feels for their child with no thought of reward. One cycle is over and before the next one begins, there is a period of light and relaxation that you can and should enjoy. Nothing is hidden and everything is out in the open, free of deception. With this card, you can be assured that nobody is trying to pull wool over your eyes.

The Sun card has links with the solar gods of world myths and legends, such as Surya in Hindu mythology, who rides a golden chariot or *rath* drawn by seven white horses and Helios in Greek mythology, who drove a chariot drawn by steeds. Throughout history, people have honoured the sun as the source of life, light and warmth. Most cultures have worshipped the sun over the ages as a giver of life, vigour, vitality and courage. The sun is the energy that makes life on earth possible. It allows crops to grow, it brings light that enables us to see things clearly without any overtones of darkness clouding our judgement. The sun is a bringer of peace after ordeals. In Tarot, The Sun card symbolizes this vitality in all its splendour.

Correspondences

The colour associated with The Sun card is golden, the planet is the sun, the herb is St John's wort, the incense is mandarin, the oils are cinnamon and orange and the gemstones are amber, citrine and golden topaz. The rune is Sowelu, which represents the power that comes from the sun's energy, and the season is summer.

The Awakening

Be bright and cheerful, happy and radiant. Happiness brings you out of the shadows to celebrate life and all its achievements. All darkness is dispelled; the night is finally over. Nothing can go wrong now.

The Shadow Aspect

This may indicate the danger of burn-out. Beware of pride and unhappiness, loneliness and lack of energy. Problems with your marriage or engagement could surface. Plans can get cancelled and there is a general uncertainty about the future. Friendships may sour or be absent from your life. Confusion and suspicion prevent you from enjoying what life has to offer.

Other Decks

In the **Mythic deck**, Apollo, the Greek sun god, is shown with a musical instrument and a pair of laurel trees, emphasizing the association of The Sun with creative arts and athletic contests.

In the **Visconti deck,** the figure wears a necklace of twelve stones indicating control over the twelve signs of the zodiac through which the sun travels every year.

Prayer

You are the Lord of light. Darkness cannot exist where you are. Then why is there so much darkness in my life? Oh Lord, bring me the light of wisdom and true knowledge so that I can discern right from wrong and live in peace with my brethren. Let me see things as they are and not as I want them to be. Bring me hope and gratitude and acceptance of Thy divine will. Let me grow spiritually and give others the unconditional love that I get from you. Let me have faith that you will bring balm to my bruised soul and that I will be taken care of. Bring me success, love and happiness.

XX
Judgement

XX. Judgement

Voice

You have been judged many times on this journey but this final judgement is for you to judge yourself. It is your evaluation and your appraisal, you are your judge and the jury. Atone if you wish, for what you find remiss is already forgiven. My clarion call is for all to get up and receive divine blessings. It is time to be born again and resurrected, cleansed and purified. The ordeal is over, the darkness has given rise to a resolution where the conscious and subconscious mind have found a meeting ground. Drop any burden that you may still bear and in your natural nakedness come to me. I am your liberation and I am your goal. Awaken to the new life that awaits you with certainty and freedom, for you have earned it. Trust your judgement and move ahead with confidence. Your assimilated knowledge and experience will show you the final leg of your journey.

Description

In this card, Angel Gabriel is shown playing an enormous trumpet. A white flag with a red cross of equal arms hangs from the trumpet, suggesting the reconciliation of opposites. Open graves are floating on the sea, with three figures standing on them, looking at the angel in awe and ecstasy. The colour of the card is grey, representing resolutions of extremes. The solar cross symbolizes balance, the four directions, four elements and the four suits of the Minor Arcana. It is a card of vindication and final solutions, of coming to terms with yourself. From the trumpet, seven notes of music emerge, the sacred music of the sphere, bringing great joy and peace to all who hear it and liberating mankind from worldly limitations. The three figures represent different stages of life. The man symbolizes the conscious mind while the woman is the subconscious and the child represents the regenerative personality. The sea is the collective unconscious from which all creations emerge and go back to. It is the stream that began in The High Priestess and is now a surging sea gaining momentum and power in its journey through all experiences till it reaches its fullness in the card of Judgement. This is the final destination—after this comes liberation. The snowy mountains in the background represent the purity of thought.

Meaning

The card of Judgement is not about condemnation, but about forgiveness of yourself and others. It is about understanding, and finding the truth. It is about making choices without blaming yourself or others. There is a feeling of relief in the card, as if a weight has been lifted from your shoulders as the passions and emotion have calmed down and there are no pretences left.

The card is about new life conquering the darkness of the grave. It is about awakening to new opportunities, which can happen when past experiences have been integrated and lessons learnt, wounds are healed and memories no longer haunt you. That is the time that you are ready to finally face the unfinished business of your life, to let go the past to move into the future that you know is peaceful and calm.

The card also indicates an inner awakening, a new way of living and experiencing the world. An unconscious knowledge or truth, which was lying dormant, is finally being awakened and brought into the light. The Judgement card has positive and negative aspects. In the positive sense, you are being awakened from a long sleep of confusion with fresh insight, psychic rebirth and resurrection. In the negative sense, you are being called to account for past actions and to justify what you have done in the past in the light of truth. It is about vindication and resolution, a chance to undo the wrong done and to prove yourself worthy of absolution. When the angel calls, you are reborn, cleansed of all guilt and burdens.

This card usually signals a big change, one that involves leaving past situations behind and stepping into something new, such as a new career. It is about letting go of something that you've been hanging on to, like a relationship or past grudges or anger. It is about forgiveness and looking at things differently. It could be a recovery after an illness or starting life afresh as a new person, unburdened by your old self.

This card represents the understanding of spiritual things, when the self is ready to bond with the universal consciousness. We understand the relationship between God and all of humanity. The coffins are dark and void of light and truth when they are closed. But here they are shown open, with the light of the angel above trumpeting the truth of the universal consciousness. This is also the card of karma, or of clearly seeing your actions and their consequences.

A new sense of joy could help you start a new life. The Judgement card promises that this new start will be positive because it is based on honesty. This card also means you will have to make a critical decision based on right and wrong, to make a choice. An honest judgement will be made, and this will have a serious impact on you.

With Pluto as its ruling planet, Judgement is about rebirth and resurrection. The idea of Judgement day is that the dead rise, their sins are forgiven and they move on to heaven. The Judgement card is similar in the sense that it asks for resurrection, to summon the past and then release it through forgiveness. There are wounds from the past that we never let heal, sins we have committed that we refuse to forgive, bad habits we haven't the courage to give up.

Finding forgiveness for yourself and others is recommended by this card. The Judgement card also suggests that you will be able to release yourself from guilt by repenting for the sins you have committed. To bring about this release, your atonement for wrongdoings in the past is required. This atonement will allow you to be freed.

This is also a card of physical healing, from an accident or illness. It can represent awakening to the call of your destiny or an effort to understand your higher purpose. It also represents a judgement in a legal matter.

Correspondences

The planet associated with the card of Judgement is Pluto, the sign is Scorpio, the colour is grey, the herb is turmeric, the oil is lime, the incense is lime verbena and the gemstones are Falcon's eye and fluorite. The rune is Kano, which is associated with fire and the inner light of wisdom that leads to good judgement.

The Awakening

All is forgiven and a new life is begun, involving reconciliation and a renewal, understanding and atonement. Evaluate past actions, know who you are and go by the flow of your new awareness and new goals.

The Shadow Aspect

Doubt about your abilities and missing new opportunities as a result can be an obstacle in your path. It could also mean failure to face facts and make the necessary changes; weakness and a feeling of disillusionment; separation and divorce.

Other Decks

In the **Renaissance deck**, a figure seen emerging from a sarcophagus represents the resurrected Christ. On the right corner is an angel and on the left corner is a sphinx, which represents rebirth and resurrection.

In the **Wirth deck,** an angel calls three figures to life so that they can continue the alchemical work of purging discontent and replacing it with optimism and a better life.

Prayer

Oh Lord, help me open my eyes and my heart so that I may perceive what is good and know what is evil. Let me atone for my sins so that when your clarion call comes I am ready to take my place in Thy heart. Let me live in this knowledge. Let me know what my destiny is and let me live in harmony with it. Let me be free of guilt and self-flagellation and secure in the knowledge that I have chosen what is right in Thy eyes. Let me be right in my judgements and make the right decision in all areas of life. Hold my hand, oh Lord, and lead me to Thy side for I am tired of the suffering in this life.

XXI
The World

XXI. The World

Voice

I am the total flowering of the senses when all limitations cease to exist. I am the liberation that comes after reconciling the opposites. I know all the colours of the rainbow. I am freedom from the self, the environment and circumstances. I have left behind all constriction and restrictions. There is no division for I am one with all. I am the dance of creation that manifests itself in everything. I am the experience that sages seek. I am the balance that seekers want. I have understood weakness and desire and hence they hold no sway over me. I am the coming together of the prakruti *and* purush, *the yin and the yang . I am the* ardh-nareshwar, *the union of the opposites, of male and female energies, in complete harmony and wholeness. I am the dynamic balance that continues creation and begins the cycle of life again.*

Description

A naked woman, draped with a purple ribbon, is in the centre of a large laurel wreath, which indicates victory. The Fool wore the same kind of laurel wreath when the journey began—as an indication of aspiring victory. His aspirations are fulfilled here. All issues are solved, all perils overcome and all lessons learnt. The World card speaks of everything coming together in fruition. It represents the completion of a journey—The Fool has finally reached his destination and is whole.

The wreath is bound together by a red ribbon forming two lemniscates or figures-of-eight, one on the top and another at the bottom of the wreath. The lemniscate is a symbol of divine energy, divine connection and protection. We have seen one lemniscate in The Magician card and another in the Strength card. The double lemniscate in The World card indicates total divine protection, presence and connection, suggesting that nothing can come between the woman and the divine.

The dancing woman is the focal point of The World card. Some suggest that she is a hermaphrodite—half-man and half-woman, the *ardh-nareshwar*—the Hindu god Shiva, who dances the cosmic dance of creation with one foot on the earth or in physical reality, the other in the cosmic world. With these connotations, the figure can be seen as symbolic of the life-giving force of creation. She holds two batons or wands in her hands, depicting the dual power that she brings to humanity. The two batons indicate that the power of The Magician has doubled as both the conscious will and the subconscious energy are balanced in this dance of abandon. Both the dance and the dancer are light and graceful. There is also a playfulness and effortlessness that is lacking in the card of The Magician. The batons also symbolize a balance; they are powerful magical instruments supporting growth both inwards and outwards.

The card represents the merging of the subconscious and the conscious, leading to the integration of both in the divine consciousness. The form of the figure is a triangle with the head, arms and legs forming the cross. The triangle above the cross indicates alchemical completion. This state of cosmic consciousness is the harmony and the unity of the mind, spirit and the soul. It is the sacred centre, which indicates the ultimate transition from the human to the divine.

The nakedness of the figure is symbolic of innocence and new beginnings—one phase is over and another is to begin. It also symbolizes dropping off all the baggage that The Fool carried in the previous cards and the final liberation from all limitations. The card of The World signifies freedom and fulfillment. It is the end of the journey, the final completion of the cycle of time. You have arrived and have accomplished your purpose.

Meaning

The Fool's journey is completed in The World, his wisdom and experience are developed to the fullest degree now. Although The World card represents achievement or completion, it is not a signal to sit back and wait for blessings to fall into your lap. This card urges you to be proactive. You must make the efforts to realize the potential that the card indicates. Focus on your heart's desire, because it is yours for the taking.

The four figures that appear in the corners of The Wheel of Fortune card, are present in the same corners of The World card. The figures in the four corners of the card represent the four fixed signs of the zodiac: Leo, Taurus, Scorpio and Aquarius. They represent the zodiac in its state of harmony, and your alignment with them. They also represent the four elements: fire is shown by the lion, earth by the bull, water by the eagle and air by the human figure. Their wings have disappeared as they have arrived at the ultimate level where no change is required.

Some experts indicate that The World card is the fourth cardinal virtue of Christianity. The other three virtues seen in the Major Arcana cards are strength, temperance and justice. The fourth virtue of wisdom is seen in The World card, represented by the woman in the centre.

The World is the card of reconciliation of the opposites. We can see the symbol of the yin and yang in the formation of the purple ribbon around the female figure. This is an oriental symbol for balance and unity of the opposites. It indicates that wholeness is achieved only when the opposites can be harmoniously blended together. It indicates acceptance and celebration of all that is different, for it is variety that adds colour to existence.

The World is the final liberation, the full understanding of inner knowledge. It is the final enlightenment that The Fool has been seeking. He now experiences the unconscious urges and thoughts. There are no limits, no boundaries, no restrictions—it is a total liberation. The World also signifies wholeness, fulfillment and blessedness. It indicates harmony and a dynamic movement for better and more exciting times. It is contentment of the heart and a feeling of satisfaction with ourselves and our lives. We seem to understand other people better, we see how everything around us is interconnected and we feel energized with a desire to work in collaboration with others on meaningful tasks and projects. The card expresses the feeling that all is well and will remain so. The World card can also indicate travel as it is through movement that The Fool has arrived at The World card.

Correspondences

The colour associated with the card of The World is purple, the colour of passion, will, royalty and knowledge. It is ruled by the planets, Saturn and Earth; the element is earth; the gemstones are lapis lazuli and amethyst. The rune is Wunjo, which signifies joy and hope and is closest to the concept of liberation and joy of The World card.

The Awakening

Dance to the rhythm of life in perfect balance and understanding. Know your inner being and be free of all restraints. When you do so, your existence is complete.

The Shadow Aspect

The time for waiting and working on yourself has come. There could be delays and frustration due to lack of vision. You may feel stifled, even trapped, but don't give up—keep a steady course for now.

Other Decks

The **Visconti deck** has two cherubs holding a globe with a vision of paradise. The four elements are also represented.

In the **Scapini deck**, the wreath the maiden wears is made up of the fruits and flowers of the earth.

Prayer

Release me from all limitations of the self and free me from all insecurities. Let me experience the wholeness that is my essence. Let me flower and grow and learn the right lessons that will bring me the freedom that I crave. Grant me the grace to see things in the right light and to give up the things that need to go. Teach me to dance to the rhythm of the universe. Let me see the harmony that lies behind all opposites and reconcile them in Thy name. Teach me to live and love with abandon and gracefully accept all that comes my way for I know that I am attracting what is necessary for my growth.

The Cards and Correspondences

Card	Colour	Herb	Oil/ perfume	Gem	Sun sign	Rune	Planet	Chakra	Hebrew letter
0 The Fool	Pale yellow	Ginseng	Galbanum	Tourmaline	Aries	Mannaz/ Wunjo	Uranus	Mooladhar or root *chakra*	Aleph
I The Magician	White	Oriental astragalus	Mace	Tiger's eye		Ansuz	Mercury		Beth
II The High Priestess	Blue	Cramp bark	Camphor	Moonstone		Lagus/ Kano	Moon	Agya or third eye *chakra*	Gimel
III The Empress	Emerald green	Chinese woman's herb, dong quai	Sage	Emerald		Fehu	Venus	Swadhistan or spleen chakra	Daleth
IV The Emperor	Orange/ Red	Ginger	Musk	Ruby		Tiewaz	Mars		Heh
V The Hierophant	Orange/ Red/ Gold	Sage	Storax	Emerald	Taurus	Othila			Waw
VI The Lovers	Orange/ Pink	Parsley	Wormwood	Rose quartz	Gemini	Gebo	Mercury		Zain
VII The Charioteer	Blue/ Yellow/ White	Dandelion	Onycha	Amber	Cancer	Ehwaz/ Kano	Moon		Cheth

Card	Colour	Herb	Oil/ perfume	Gem	Sun sign	Rune	Planet	Chakra	Hebrew letter
VIIII Strength	Yellow/ White	Cayenne	Oilbanum	Cetrine	Leo	Uruz/ Wunjo/ Thyrisaz	Sun		Teth
IX The Hermit	Grey/ Yellow-green	Liquorice	Mace	Topaz	Virgo	Perdhro/ Algiz			Yod
X Wheel of Fortune	Purple	Slippery elm	Saffron	Sapphire		Jera/ Raido	Jupiter		Kaph
XI Justice	Green	Plantain	Galbanum	Blood stone	Libra	Thyrisaz / Nauthiz	Venus		Lamed
XII The Hanged Man	Blue	Irish moss or kelp	Myrrh	Aquamarine		Perth/ Nied	Neptune		Mem
XIIII Death	Blue-green	Elder-flower	Asafoetida	Black tourmaline	Scorpio	Eihwaz			Nun
XIV Temperance	Blue	Echinacea	Sandal wood	Rose quartz, aquamarine	Sagittarius	Ingwaz		Anahata or heart *chakra*	Samekh

XV The Devil	Black	Lobella	Nutmeg	Black onyx	Capricorn	Nauthiz	Earth		Ayin
XVI The Tower	Scarlet red	Garlic	Pepper	Garnet		Hagalaz	Mars		Peh
XVII The Star	Pale yellow/ Blue	Star anise/ Skullcap	Rosewood/ Galbanum	Turquoise/ aquamarine	Aquarius	Dagaz		Vishuddhi or throat *chakra*	Tzaddi
XVIII The Moon	Silver	Valerian	Lemon grass	Moonstone	Pisces/ Cancer	Isa	Moon		Qoph
XIX The Sun	Golden	St John's wort	Orange/ Cinnamon	Amber / citrine/ golden topaz		Sowelu	Sun	Manipur chakra or solar plexus	Resh
XX Judgement	Grey	Turmeric	Lime oil	Falcon's eye/ fluorite		Kano	Pluto		Shin
XII The World	Violet	Comfrey	Frankincense	Lapis lazuli/ amethyst		Wunjo	Saturn / Earth	Sahasrar or crown *chakra*	Tau

Chapter Three

True Stories

3.

True Stories

The stories narrated in this chapter are all based on the authentic experiences of clients who have come to me. I have, of course, taken the utmost care to camouflage the identity of each client.

The reason that I have so much material is that initially, I was not very sure of the oracle and had to prove to myself that it really worked. There was a dichotomy in my life, a conflict of head and heart, due to my being born on the cusp of Libra–Scorpio, which meant that two different aspects were pulling in opposite directions. The investigative Scorpio needed a deeper knowledge of and a stronger connection to Tarot in order to accept the oracle, while the cognitive Libra had to be convinced rationally.

I kept a Tarot journal with details of clients who came to me, what they asked, what the cards said, which cards appeared, what advice I had given and how the problem was or was not resolved.

All I asked of my clients was to get back to me with information about how the events unfolded. Most of them gave me feedback, allowing me to look at my interpretations afresh and learn from the mistakes that I made.

My journal recorded not only case studies, which are interesting to know about and learn from, and also heart-warming and sometimes painful stories. The stories are a peep into the lives of real people with real issues that they grapple with in silence.

I have chosen stories that will be of interest to readers and that were resolved in a striking way. In some cases, the Tarot advice did not work out. Sometimes, the reason for a dead-end was my own disturbed mental state at the relevant time, where I was not able to connect to the right meaning of the cards. In hindsight, I could decipher the reasons why this happened. In other cases, my desire to predict positive things superseded my neutrality, resulting in the wrong answers because they reflected my emotions, instead of the wisdom of Tarot. These results taught me that if you want the right answers, objectivity and balance are very important. It is essential to be detached while reading the cards and to have the courage to accept what the cards say. Emotions get in the way of correctly interpreting the cards. Lies, deceit or trying to trip the cards by evasion does not give you any tissue answers.

In rare cases, I have been truly mystified as to why Tarot did not work but that, I suppose, is God's will and a way of showing that He is in control and chooses to operate through us. I hope you enjoy the stories.

1. The Beautician Who Found Her Mother

This story is from my early experiences of Tarot, many years before satellite television and mobile phones. The world was far-flung and travelling to another country was only possible for the elite few. India was still a closed country beset by ignorance and poverty, unable to cope with her teeming problems. To the average Indian, Europe seemed frightening and remote, unknown and sophisticated. It was at this time that a beautician came to me with a strange story. She was the daughter of an English mother and an Indian Maharaja, who threw the Englishwoman out after she delivered his child. Not only that, out of spite, he forcibly took away the baby from the mother. It was at the time of Partition in India and the Englishwoman had no other choice but to go back to England, leaving the little girl behind.

Once the Maharaja's purpose of making the Englishwoman suffer was served, he did not want to have anything to do with the child. So he put her in an orphanage and forgot about her. The girl was subsequently adopted by a loving couple, but grew up with a desperate longing to find her mother. She had nothing to go by, except a name and some idea of her mother's age. She had no money, no friends and no one to help her. As she narrated her story, tears began to stream down her face. I took out my cards and we did a number of spreads. As I read the cards, it emerged that she would get help in finding her mother from her workplace—a client of hers and a blond man, would assist her and within three months, she would be able to contact her mother. To me, this sounded a little too optimistic, even improbable, but we let it go at that. She went away and I let the matter rest. One day, I received a frantic call from the beautician, urgently requesting me to come to her beauty parlour. She showed me a letter, which had arrived about two-and-a-half months after the reading. It was from her mother!

How had this turn of events come about? Some of her clients were to travel abroad and had kindly consented to help her. They agreed to hire a detective in England to search for her mother and were even willing to take the payment for the detective in installments and in Indian rupees. As it happens, the detective who managed to find the mother was a blond man! My friend was all set to go abroad at her mother's invitation and meet her long-lost parent.

2. The Judge Who Came from Dehradun

One day, a retired high court judge from Dehradun came to see me. He was small-built, frail and old and was terrified of death, but he had a razor-sharp mind. His health was his primary concern.

He had come to Mumbai for his hernia operation and as both his son and daughter-in-law were officers in the Indian Administrative Services in the city, he had access to the best doctors. His family wanted him to get the operation done immediately, as it was a fairly simple one, but he wanted his heart specialist to be with him during the operation. His heart specialist was touring as a part of the President's retinue of doctors at the time so waiting for him meant a delay, which his son did not want. The demanding old man must have been a difficult person to live with, fretting and fuming like a caged lion in a small apartment in Mumbai, away from his house in Dehradun.

He wanted me to ask the cards whether all would go well with his the operation and, more importantly, whether he should have it without his heart specialist or wait for him to come back from his tour. His spread showed that the operation would be successful, but it also showed some minor technical complications, which is why I advised him not to have the operation without his heart specialist.

About a month later, I came home to find flowers, fruit and a large box of *mithai* waiting for me. The retired judge sat in my living room with tears in his eyes and with folded hands. He said that I had saved his life. During his operation the anaesthetist had given a slight overdose of anesthesia, which made the old man's heart stop, but instant treatment by the heart specialist had saved his life.

After that incident, he became a permanent feature in my life. He called me Doctor *sahiba* and called me on the phone every week from Dehradun to share his innermost thoughts and worries, such as his daughter's marriage, his money and estate and consulted me before taking any major decision, to the extent that his dependence on me began to worry me. Then, suddenly, his calls stopped. I felt a little anxious, but had no way of contacting him.

3. 'My Husband Wants to Kill Me...'

The operator in my office buzzed me to say that a lady had come to meet me. Usually I did not meet people without an appointment as I always had a busy schedule. But when the operator spoke to me on the phone, something in the tone of her voice made me pause and say that I would come out to the foyer to see her. I had no clue what the lady might want from me. Was it a visa problem? Some scholarship request? An urgent funding need? I had always managed to keep my office life completely separate from my Tarot work. Not many people knew where I worked and I had been successful in compartmentalizing my life, so I did not expect someone to come to my office for Tarot. I was also a little irritated as I had to leave some important work incomplete to attend to this person.

It was almost closing time. I took a deep breath and as I walked into the foyer, I saw a stylish, well-groomed young woman waiting for me. I said, 'I believe you are waiting to see me.' She silently handed me her card. She held an impressive post in a reputed advertising company. She removed her dark glasses and looked at me. I was startled—her eyes were vacant and devoid of any emotion. With a deadpan look she said dully, 'My husband wants to kill me,' and silently stared at me. I did not know how to react, so I merely stared back. I asked her to wait and went in to collect my things. We drove home in silence and

I offered her a glass of water and some tea. She accepted both meekly.

Slowly, the story came out. She came from a dysfunctional family—her parents did not value their children and both she and her brother felt like orphans. They did not want her in the house, making it clear that she should become independent as early as possible and leave them in peace. She was an Aries and her emotional, attention-seeking outbursts labelled her as mentally unstable. She was not sociable and did not have any friends. She met her husband at her workplace and they got married almost immediately. After her marriage, her parents cut all ties with her, while her brother migrated to Australia. Her widowed mother-in-law, a very domineering woman who had a strong influence on her son, stayed with them. Soon after her marriage, she realized that the mother-in-law had a lover who visited her at night. He was rumoured to have an underworld connection and everyone in the locality was scared of him. The son was aware of this but chose not to interfere with his mother's life.

Quarrels soon began, both with her mother-in-law and husband. One night, she heard her mother-in-law tell the husband that it would be best to get rid of his wife and that she would find him someone richer and much better-looking. She could not hear her husband's reply, but she was shocked and terrified. She loved her husband but knew that he was a weak man who could very easily get influenced and swayed. When he was with her he would listen to her, but when he was with his mother he would do as she said. Then she overheard them planning to use kerosene to burn her and the next day, she saw her husband with a big tin of kerosene. The lover started visiting more frequently and the atmosphere in the house became even more oppressive, giving her sleepless nights. In desperation, she contacted a woman's organization down the street. She confided in them but their interference only made matters worse. They were threatened with dire consequences and the husband denied that he had had any such conversation with his mother.

Despite this trauma, my friend could not leave her marital home. That was the real problem. Rationally, she knew what she needed to do but emotionally, she could not leave her husband. She was psychologically incapable of disentangling herself. Her new home was the only security that she had known in her life and she could not let it go. Despite her fear for her life, she continued to stay with her husband. What she needed was emotional support but there was no one to help her—her parents did not wish to be troubled and her brother was far away. To make matters worse, she lost her job because of major behavioural problems resulting from the pressure of her circumstances, her fears and her emotions.

Her problems were on several levels and took a long time to unravel. The most important, positive outcome of the readings we did was that she got a new job. We identified the right company from the three that she had short-listed and she began working again. Further, the cards assured her that there was no immediate threat from her husband and mother-in-law—the woman's organization had created a stink so she was safe. This calmed her considerably.

We identified areas of self-development and got her started on meditation, chanting and clearing her karma. She was advised to start consulting a counsellor, which she did. The solution the cards offered was a separation, followed by a divorce. They also indicated that it would take time. She needed to build up her strength and only then proceed with a separation or else it would not work.

The consultation continued over a long period of time and the cards indicated the next steps until finally, she was able to move out to her own flat, file for a separation and a divorce.

The last time I heard from her, she was in Singapore, doing extremely well for herself. I hope that she has continued to follow the advice of the cards, which indicated that she was to heal and strengthen her scarred mind completely before getting involved with another man.

4. The Lover Who Lied

A woman I knew was involved with a married man for ten years, an important man in the corporate world. He would meet her at his convenience—sometimes he would come to her regularly and at other times, stop all contact with her for a long time and then without warning, restart the relationship. This pattern continued for a long time and this woman's entire life was spent waiting for him. He kept her on a string, which she hung on to precariously. Even though she had a good job and several marriage offers, she had eyes for no one else, living in the hope that one day things would change and he would marry her. His own marriage was dead—there was nothing between him and his wife, except money and a power game that she played with him. The wife did not want to leave the security of her marital home. She had a position in society, all the comforts in the world and a circle of friends that she was happy with. When she suspected him of having a relationship outside the marriage, she even hired a private detective to follow him and in those months, he did not dare to call my friend. He was terrified of exposure, as he had a lot to lose. If the scandal broke, the shares of his company would come crashing down and all the status and wealth he had so painstakingly accumulated would collapse. He could not afford the alimony as his wife, an aggressive and wily woman, would want her full pound of flesh, which would destroy him. She was also involved in his business and that complicated the matter further.

When I did readings for my friend, the spreads indicated that her lover would never leave his wife, no matter what he said. My friend was very disappointed and refused to accept the possibility that he would not marry her, especially since many astrologers had told her that the relationship would work out. She had all her plans in place: what she would do after she had married him, where they would live, what kind of household she would run and how she would take care of him.

She kept making excuses for him when he stayed away, and when his absence became unbearable, she would swallow her pride and call him. She truly loved him and would have made a wonderful, devoted wife to some lucky man. The man was not a villain either—he was just too weak to stand up to his wife and end his marriage.

Every two to three months, my friend would come for a reading, saying that things had changed and she felt that he was on the verge of telling his wife about her and asking for a divorce. But the cards told a different story. On several occasions, I tried to tell her the truth gently but she was not open to it. She would at once refer to an astrologer who had given her definite dates of an improvement in her situations. I, too, hoped against hope that things would change and kept reading cards for her. This situation went on for many years until, one day, the man abruptly stopped answering her calls and severed all connection with her.

Despite all my warnings, it was a great shock to my friend. I am sure she realized that I had been right all along, although I was sorry that I could not tell her anything positive. Her whole life was wasted because this weak, selfish man could not tell her the truth, that he would never divorce his wife. She was so unhappy that she moved away to another city. I often hope that, perhaps, she has met another man, that she is married now and is living a fulfilled life, instead of facing the loneliness she was left with.

5. The Lady Who Vanished

In the early days of my Tarot work, a family friend brought a Parsi gentleman to me. He must have been in his thirties and was boyish-looking, with a pleasing countenance and easy manners. He was very distraught and came straight to the point. His elderly mother had disappeared two days ago and he wanted to find her as soon as possible. He asked me if I could help him find her. His mother, he said, was getting senile and was prone to behaving in an erratic and impulsive fashion. She had tried to run away from the house earlier, but had been intercepted by a watchful nurse. This time she had been cleverer. She had waited for her nurse to doze off in the afternoon after lunch, and had quietly slipped away without anyone noticing her disappearance until much later.

Unfortunately, she was wearing a lot of gold jewellery, which she could sell to do or get whatever she wanted. The son was worried about her safety. She had been fretting to go see her daughter, but because of her ill health the son had not allowed her to do so. It was difficult to get her to travel as she was quite unpredictable, but this time, the spirited old woman had decided to take matters into her own hands. The family did not want to go to the police just yet. Theirs was a well-known Parsi family and the son was worried that it would endanger the mother more if the information about who she was leaked out. The press would not only have a field day and rake up a terrible scandal, but she would become an easy prey for kidnapping and extortion.

He had contacted all his relatives, including his sister, but they had no information about her. He had come to me as a last resort, fully prepared to contact the police and flash her photograph all over the city should it not work. He was aware of the risk but felt that there was no other option.

We did a number of spreads. The first spread indicated that she was safe and secure—the Nine of Pentacles assured me of that.

The next spread showed a number of movement cards like the Six of Swords, the Knight of Pentacles and Cups, indicating that she had travelled. The transaction card of Six of Pentacles had also appeared, showing that the son's fear that she had sold her jewellery was not unfounded.

Then, although finding directions is not easy in Tarot, we got an indication that she had travelled north. The son could not think of anyone or anywhere that she could go to in north India. The cards also revealed that they would get information about her or she would contact them in a couple of days and that he should not worry. All would end well.

Although the son was not satisfied, he decided to go with the cards' advice and wait for a couple of days before contacting the police. I was worried because, though I had tried to help him to the best of my knowledge, I did not want his mother's life to be jeopardized by the delay in contacting the police.

I heard nothing from him until the fourth day, when I came home to find a basket of flowers and a box of chocolates. There was a note saying, 'You were right! My mother was found in Chandigarh where one of her dear friends lives. We had completely forgotten about her. She called from Chandigarh and my brother is bringing my mother back today.'

Later I was told that she had sold her necklace for a pittance to buy a train ticket to Chandigarh. As there was no direct train, she had changed trains with the help of strangers in Delhi and safely reached Chandigarh! She had phoned her friend who picked her up from the station and, realizing what the old lady had done, called the family.

This was one of my earliest cases that ended well. I was still a novice and the outcome helped build my confidence in the oracle.

6. Taken for a Ride

In the early days of our marriage, my husband was looking for an opportunity to start a new business venture. He did not have much experience and was looking for a partner who would work with him in the field of computers. We were new to Mumbai and did not have many friends. We met a girl who said that she had studied computer science in the US. She had worked there for a long time but had come back because of a broken relationship and to look after her widowed mother. She seemed fun-loving and capable and easily slipped into the role of a family friend and confidante. She had a fantastic proposal for international trade and was willing to take on the full responsibility for that side of the business. She seemed a perfect fit—an extrovert, who got along easily with everyone she met while my husband was an introvert, and both were interested in computers. We signed a partnership deed and embarked upon the venture. She seemed a godsend and we accepted her as a business partner with a sigh of relief.

The partnership began very well. But slowly, nagging doubts about her crept in. For instance, she insisted that there had been discussions that my husband said were non-existent, some decisions that she took without consulting him and cheques that were signed in his absence.

These were my early days with Tarot and I sought the wisdom of the oracle. I got the card of The Devil in the result position. The Devil represents deceit, lies, mental distortions, recklessness and indulgence of the senses. I did not understand the implication of the card and consequently did not relate it to her or our business. Soon, my husband and I were fighting about silly things, and small misunderstandings began to spoil our relationship. For instance, she would not pass on my messages to my husband when I called, and lied about his whereabouts. Projects that depended on her technical expertise got delayed or derailed, but the explanations were glib and so convincing that we never doubted her.

The business was going downhill and so was our personal relationship. Slowly, I started making enquiries and finally met someone who knew her. The truth came out—she did not have a computer degree. She exploited unsuspecting people by winning their trust and spinning tales and no one suspected her because most people did not check out the credentials she claimed to have.

To extricate ourselves meant financial loss that we could ill afford, but more importantly, we discovered how easy it was to create a misunderstanding between married couples if they were not alert. She created a wedge by reporting things that were slightly distorted and difficult for us to verify—we did not even try for we felt that she had no ulterior motive. I trusted her so much that I was willing to leave my six-year-old son in her care—although thankfully I did not. Finally, my husband politely told her that he could not work with her. It was very difficult for him but he did it. We accepted our losses and heaved a sigh of relief once she was out of our lives.

We often go through negative experiences because of our weakness and our karma. My husband and I learnt the hard way not to trust others immediately and to trust each other more. Also, we realized that it is so easy to damage a relationship if you are not careful and there is not enough communication.

Most of all, I learnt to trust the cards and take their guidance seriously.

7. Speculators

I have some friends who are keen speculators. They bet on anything from the weather forecast to sports. They have often tried to involve me and my Tarot cards in their speculation, which I have resisted strongly. They have even offered me a percentage in their winnings! I never accepted such offers as I do not believe that Tarot should be used for betting or gambling. To me, Tarot is for healing, for improving human existence, to help people understand themselves better and to connect with their inner beings for a happier life. It is an instrument for counselling and to find the right direction when you are at a crossroad in your life. My friends laugh at me for being so impractical, but on the whole, they respect my sentiments and refrain from involving me in any of their nefarious plans. They have been my clients as well and I have helped them in their personal lives. Since they have benefited from Tarot consultation, they have a regard for the esoteric science.

One year, during the Cricket World Cup series, the whole country was in the grip of cricket mania. The final match—between India and Australia—was pure nail-biting, nerve-wracking suspense. It was almost a war as fans betted insanely about the winner of the World Cup all over cities and towns. There was nothing more important than the outcome of the match and bookies and speculators were having a field day. Though I am not a cricket enthusiast, I come from a cricket-loving family and both my father and brother were Ranji Trophy players. My knowledge of cricket is limited to random facts picked up inadvertently over the years. Despite attempts by my father to instil a love for cricket in my sister and I, we remained indifferent.

But this match was different and even I was caught up in the excitement. The night before the final match between India and

Australia, very high stakes were being played. My friend, in a spurt of national pride, placed a huge bet in favour of India winning the World Cup. He called me and told me what he had done. It was a big gamble and though he did not directly ask me to help him through Tarot, I felt pressurized and worried.

For a while, I held on to my resolve as I did not want to get blackmailed into using Tarot for any commercial purpose or to save him from any foolish bet he had consciously chosen to place. By 10 p.m. that night, however, my resolve weakened and I was worried. By 11 p.m., I was unable to stop myself, and against my better judgement, I did a spread for my own satisfaction, just to know who would win the World Cup the next day.

The cards were quite clear—India would lose the World Cup to Australia! I frantically called up my friend and asked him to cancel the bet, explaining what the cards said. He promptly did just that. The rest is history. Many people lost a lot of money the next day, but my friend was not one of them. I felt good that I had been able to save at least one misguided person from disaster.

The next day, my friend called me and thanked me. I told him that I hoped he had learnt his lesson. He said that he wished he had listened to me before, adding that he actually had only cancelled the bet. If he had not been so surprised by my hysteria, he would have taken the full advice and not only cancelled the bet on India, but would have placed the bet on Australia and won a fortune! As they say, a leopard never changes its spots.

8. 'I Want to Kill Myself. . .'

A well-known model appeared on my doorstep without an appointment, desperate for advice. Fortunately, she came after my last client had left. I was tired but seeing her desperation, I relented. I made her sit down in my living room while I went in to freshen up. I anticipated a long session!

I came back to find her staring vacantly at a picture. She was gorgeous—tall, slim, stylishly made-up and smartly dressed. She looked every inch the successful model that she was. She had a charming smile, but there was something very dismal about her, a hint of recklessness and a slight distortion in her eyes. She came straight to the point. 'I tried to kill myself last week and I still feel the urge to do it again. Can you help me?'

After soothing her, I asked her to tell me her story. She came from a conservative family in a small town, where moral restrictions and segregation were the norm. She had studied in a girl's college and boyfriends were unthinkable. She was tall for her age and people made fun of her height, not appreciating her potential attractiveness. In fact, her father talked openly and degradingly about her looks, saying that no one would marry her as she was too dark and lanky, which were cruel words for a growing child to take.

While in college, she met someone connected with the fashion world so she ran away from home and started a career in modelling. Her father filed a case against her for stealing her mother's jewellery, which increased the great bitterness between her and her family members. She had not seen them in several years and had no connection with them.

Meanwhile, she went through a trail of failed relationships, getting into one toxic relationship after another. She was doing well professionally but her personal life was hell. Lonely and isolated, she hankered for her family and the secure (though shackled) life she had left behind. She was terrified of her father and did not dare to approach her family for help.

She had discovered, sadly, and a little late, that she believed in the very values that she had scoffed at and left behind in her hometown. It made her feel terrible about what she had become. Deep down, she was embarrassed by the vicious cycle of drinking, smoking and temporary relationships that she had gotten into. She hated herself but did not know how to stop or retrace her steps. She no longer knew who she was and how to get connected with herself. She did not belong anywhere.

When we did some spreads, the card of the Hermit appeared prominently, indicating the need for her to turn inwards through meditation. I advised her to take up any self-development programme that suited her. The Hermit also indicated the need for expert guidance and I suggested the intervention of a good psychiatrist who would help. I also asked her to meditate on the card of The Hermit, as it would help her to connect with herself. Her next spread indicated that one of her sisters, represented by the Queen of Wands, was sympathetic towards her so I asked her to get in touch with her discreetly. This was a big hurdle, as her fear of rejection prevented her from making the contact, but eventually she did and the sister responded positively.

As she had enough money, I asked her to quit modelling and take a break to sort through her problems so that she could lighten the burden of guilt and shame that was corroding her. It was not about right or wrong. It was about her psyche and her belief system. She was operating against her own beliefs and the result was a mental dichotomy.

She followed the advice and took a break. She became more at peace with herself and her erratic behaviour patterns, her bouts of drunkenness, her depression and self-destructive behaviour slowly faded. Though there were bad days, her life came back on track. The big breakthrough was her sister's support, which gave her an emotional anchor and a connection to her past.

In a spread related to her profession, the Page of Cups card appeared prominently, which indicated her interest in the arts, and with further probing, we discovered that she had always been interested in interior design. With my encouragement, over the next six months she did a short course in interior design and began doing small assignments that kept her occupied. The cards had advised her get out of her self-destructive relationship with her current boyfriend and with the help of her sister's emotional support, she was able to do this too.

As she went through the process of mending her life, we kept in touch and after a year, the cards indicated that she should meet her parents. The sister spoke to them about her and prepared the ground. The first meeting was very awkward but the father did not turn away. That was the beginning and gradually, she was welcome back by her family. It was a hard climb but she made it.

Her problem was her inability to handle her father's rejection. Her rebellion stemmed from the hurt and the humiliation that made her break away from her family and the world that she belonged to. She did things to spite them, forgetting that she was also hurting herself. She did not really believe in her actions and the resulting conflict almost killed her. Today, I hear she is a married woman with a family of her own and I hope she has found happiness at last.

9. Castles in the Air

A Muslim gentleman (from the Bohri community) came to see me, seeking advice about a business opportunity in Russia. A part of the deal was that he had to marry the daughter of the family that was offering the chance to improve his fortunes. He said that he saw no reason not to use this marriage to augment his career. This sounded a little mercenary to me, but I agreed to do spreads for him. During the reading, the two cards that came up repeatedly were The Devil and the Knight of Cups reversed. This did not augur well for the marriage or for the enterprise. We tried several different combinations and permutations, but the advice of the cards was to avoid both. However, he was honest enough to say that he did not wish to miss the opportunity to start a business in Russia. I wished him luck and he went away. I felt disturbed as it seemed from the cards that he was getting into trouble. He was a nice enough man, quite straightforward and frank, but the cards had warned of deceit, lies and immorality. The Knight of Cups reversed indicated that the proposal should be carefully scrutinized before accepting it. Something was seriously wrong.

I had asked this client to let me know how things worked out as I wanted to know what became of him and whether the cards were right. I received his wedding card so I knew that he had gone ahead with the deal. I often wondered about him, but there was no way of contacting him and so I forgot about him for a while. Almost a year later, I received a phone call from him and he came to see me again. He looked subdued and very quiet. He began by saying that he had walked into a trap. It seemed that the girl had disfiguring blemishes on her body, which he discovered only after the marriage. Furthermore, she was not educated and had no social graces.

After the marriage, the father-in-law made a big show of setting up meetings for him in Russia, but when my client went to Russia with his hard-earned funds, he discovered to his horror that it was all a farce. No meetings came through because the names and addresses provided to him were merely taken from a directory, not through personal contacts. He came back a broken man. He had lost all his money and his small business in India had also suffered in his absence. His father-in-law made feeble excuses, but he divorced his wife, threatening the family with legal action if they even mentioned the *meher* money.

He had learnt a hard lesson. He had tried to take advantage of a family to realize his ambitions, but was exploited in turn. The lesson for him was that there are no short cuts in life. Now, he is a bachelor and is thankful that he has been able to stabilize his hardware business.

10. Deception

A man and a woman came to me, saying they were siblings and wanted to seek advice from the Tarot regarding the woman's marriage problems. Her husband was irresponsible, came home late and ill-treated her. They wanted to know what the future of the marriage was. As I only did one-to-one counselling, I asked the brother to step into another room. Surprisingly, I met with resistance and he said that he needed to be there as he was very concerned. I explained how in Tarot, the answers well up from the deep unknown and the answers that emerge are certainly not meant to be shared. They were only meant for the querent and no one else. I managed to convince him that interference from the vibration of another person would retract from the reading, so he reluctantly agreed to go.

I started doing the spreads with the woman, who started with a question. The cards that came up in the spread were negative and in the result position, I got the card of the Knight of Cups reversed. This suggested immorality and the advice to consider the proposal carefully. This card had no connection with her question. We tried again but the cards were random and did not make any sense—they appeared as The Lovers reversed, The Charioteer reversed, The Devil, the Page of Cups reversed and the Eight of Swords. All these cards relate to unethical victory, unfaithfulness, deceit and lies. This did not fit in with anything that the woman had said. I was perplexed and kept asking probing questions, based on the cards, but saw her get visibly upset. She began to cry and the truth came out. The man with her was not her brother but her lover! She really wanted to know how she could divorce her husband and marry her lover. She said her husband was ineffectual, but the cards revealed the real issue—unfaithfulness.

She had two children. They had appeared reversed in the Page of Cups, which meant that the lover did not want them. She was not aware of this because he had lied, saying that he would accept the children. We talked about it and it was clear that she would never leave them. When we confronted her lover with his true intentions, he was taken aback and in that split second she realized that the cards were right. She was a woman caught in her own web, a weak woman who had been sweet-talked into an affair, into a life of deceit, lies and unfaithfulness. The husband did not know about her infidelity, at least not yet.

I told her frankly that she had to make her own decision. Unless she was honest with herself, she would not be able to find the right solution to her problem. She had to see herself as she really was, look at her weaknesses and understand her own needs. No one would be able to help her, except herself. By now she was sobbing openly—she did not know what to do, she loved her children, but found her husband unattractive. She was sexually active and wanted a partner who would satisfy her, but was torn between her sexual needs and her children. Her dilemma was certainly not the fault of her husband, who was not the wicked man they had painted him to be.

The cards had revealed that this impasse would not continue and that her unfaithfulness would soon be discovered. It would be better for her to take the decision now and stick with it. The cards had also revealed that the children would not be allowed to go with her if she left her marital home. It was a difficult choice but she had to make it. She had learnt something about her lover that she had not known and realized her real need and love for her children. I don't know what decision she finally took. I hope she had the good sense to see what the cards had implied. I felt sorry for her because her desire had overpowered her, but she was not an unconventional woman who could have braved public opinion and gone with her lover, nor was she a moral housewife who could sacrifice her needs for the family. What was the right choice for her? And what did she actually do? I will never know for she did not get back to me again.

11. More Than Meets the Eye

One day, a handsome man from a well-known family in Mumbai came to see me. He was married with two children, but told me that he was in love with another person and wanted to know how to solve this dilemma. Being somewhat reticent, he did not mention any names.

We did a few spreads. The Queen of Cups appeared and he recognized her as his wife, who was his problem. His other family members appeared in the spreads—a powerful mother, a successful father, a clever younger brother—all came up in relevant places with correct descriptions. But I could not get any details about the woman he loved. The cards were silent and I could not find any links or connections. Where was the beloved and why did she not appear in any of the spreads? I was baffled and did not have an answer. What I got instead was the card of The Lovers, the card of choice; the card of The Tower, meaning a feeling of being trapped; The Devil, representing sexuality, and finally, the card of the Hierophant reversed, which indicated unconventionality!

With this card, a nebulous suspicion of the nature of the problem dawned on me. What had put me off the track was that he was married with two children! In those days, people did not talk openly about their sexual preference. The Knight of Swords had appeared in a prominent place and I asked him who it referred to. I described him as a good-looking, clean-hearted, aggressive young man. He looked sheepish and did not meet my eye. He mumbled, 'He is the person I love.'

Despite the inkling I had, I was taken aback. It was the first time I had seen homosexuality in such a conventional garb! Tears were pouring down the man's face. He was mortified and in great pain because of the constant conflict. He came from a very conventional background and did not know what to do. He had tried to suppress his sexual preference all his life, but could not resist it after meeting the Knight of Swords. The cards now made sense. It also meant that he had a choice. He could continue to pretend to be a heterosexual and carry on his homosexual activities in secret, which was an easier path for him as it did not mean a drastic change of lifestyle or social exposure. This subterfuge was, of course, very unfair to the wife who had a right to expect the love of a husband. The alternative was to break the shackles of convention, come out of The Tower and start living with his lover.

Both these options were unacceptable to him. We asked the oracle again for guidance. The third option that emerged was to take his wife into confidence and leave the decision to her. If she chose to live within the marriage, he would need to facilitate the pretence. If she chose to leave him, then he would need to fulfill his responsibility towards her and take care of her.

He agreed to try the third option and came back after a few days to say that unfair as it was, the wife had opted to stay within the marriage and wanted him to maintain a decent façade at all times. He could conduct his relationship discreetly, but never publicly humiliate her by revealing that he was homosexual. She would expect him to support her in every possible way. If she found a suitable match, he agreed he would gracefully divorce her and let her marry again. From his side, he offered her the option of conducting a discreet liaison while staying within the marriage.

The cards indicated that the children should not be affected by the situation, so he and his wife decided to send them to a boarding school.

Since then, I have met him socially many times and his peaceful expression tells me that things have worked out for him. My biggest fear was for his children—how they would react when they found out the truth about their parents?

12. Looks are Deceptive

I once met a glamorous woman at a party. Glittering with diamonds, she seemed to have everything—she was beautiful, stylish and confident. Most people knew her as she was married into one of the well-known families of Mumbai. She exuded power and wealth and she had two children. What more could one want?

As we talked, she revealed an interest in Tarot and asked for an appointment. I was surprised. We agreed to meet the following week and I wondered through the week what this gorgeous woman could possibly want to know. She had told me that hers was a love marriage. She was working in a five star hotel when her husband saw her and they had married within six months of their meeting. It all sounded so romantic.

She came promptly at the appointed hour dressed in a shell-pink *salwar kurta*, with a row of pearls on her neck and a cream clutch bag that matched her shoes. Her smile was warm. After the usual pleasantries, I asked her what she wanted to consult the oracle for. For a moment there was silence. Then with a sigh, she said, 'I have been married for eighteen hellish years. My son is seventeen and my daughter is sixteen. Both are terrified of their father, who is capable of lashing them with his belt and traumatizing them in various ways. He has done this many times in the past, whenever he wanted to get even with me. Just two years after our marriage, I discovered that he had a mistress whom he had no intention of giving up.' He said that he had 'honoured' my friend by offering marriage to her and giving her children. He had given her money, jewellery, a position in society. What more could she want? Why should she interfere with his life? My friend was shocked and horrified and wanted to go back to her own sane middle-class home with the children.

But what her husband said made her freeze. He said that if she tried to get away from him or file for a divorce, he would ensure that she never saw her children again. He would fight her in every court and use all his influence to deprive her of what she loved the most. He wanted her to maintain appearances and continue living in the house as his wife because it suited him to have her there to maintain a social façade. She could not take up a job as it was not appropriate for a woman of her position. 'What could I do?' my friend sadly said. 'I had no money, no job and no way of getting my children out of his clutches. He did not want them but he was not going to let me have them either. My in-laws refused to help.' So she stayed on, moved into the spare bedroom and tried to raise the children to the best of her abilities in this terrible situation. She kept her children away from him as he humiliated them for no reason.

Years went by and she learnt to keep up appearances. She also managed to do many online courses and earned impressive degrees from prestigious universities abroad. She had come to me because she had reached a cross-roads in her life. Her younger brother had moved to the US and had got US citizenship. He had applied for her citizenship as well, which was likely to come through soon, and was asking her to leave her husband and move to the US. He was willing to support her and the children. What was she to do? She wanted to be free, but was worried about the backlash. Her husband was a vengeful and a powerful man and she was worried that he would harm her children.

We did some spreads for her. The first card that came up was Death, implying that change was brewing in her life and if she handled it well, she would experience a complete turnaround in her circumstances. The other card that came up was the Six of Swords, suggesting travel and a change in consciousness. The card of The Sun was prominently placed, which meant happiness and success. What emerged from more spreads was that she should not be impatient, but wait for a while. She was advised to send the children off to a boarding school in the US first. Only once they were settled there, should she move off to the US as well, not before or else her husband would leave no stone unturned to stop her. It was important that the children were moved out of the father's sphere of influence, to a place where he could not touch them or he would use them to thwart her plans and keep her tied to him. It was important that the plan be kept a closely guarded secret.

The cards were clear that this was the best option, for once the children were out of India, he would be powerless to stop them, and by the time he knew what was going on, the son would turn eighteen, an adult beyond his father's control and the daughter would be close to turning eighteen as well. My friend went away with some hope in her heart, but still terrified about the plan.

After she left, I sat down, totally shocked. I could not believe that appearances could be so deceptive. Years later, she came to meet me. After giving me a warm hug, she told me that the plan had worked out for her as predicted by the cards. Her children were now working in the US, and she had a wonderful job. I was happy to see that she looked contented and even more glamorous than ever.

13. It Was Never to Be ...

A young friend came to me, wanting to know when she would get married. Her father had passed away and she did not get on very well with her mother and had spent much of her childhood in hostels, which may have been the reason for her craving for love and affection. Very emotional and loyal, she could smother the object of her affection with her adoration, dependence and her need. She was popular and could easily make friends, but needed a deeper commitment in relationships that perhaps was hard to come by. She had a good job and earned well too, but her fervent wish was to get married and when this failed to materialize, she had bouts of depression, fear and loneliness. She asked me to consult the cards to know when she would get married. I, too, thought that marriage was a solution for her as a husband and children would give her the emotional security she was seeking. I encouraged her to find a life partner—but nothing seemed to work for her.

We did spreads for her on a regular basis, but the cards were either silent or negative. She tried matrimonial columns to find a match for herself and even came close to getting engaged. At the time, we did her reading with excitement and got Three of Cups reversed, which is not a good card for any kind of celebration—and sure enough, at the last minute, her fiance called off the wedding. Slowly, she began to change, becoming uncommunicative and distant. She was living in a hostel and her visits became less frequent. I confess that it was perhaps my fault that I could not give her the attention that she needed. I was completely swamped by circumstances since I had a demanding job and also had to look after my very young son and my father, who went through a near-fatal illness—all of which left me completely drained. I was involved in my own problems.

One day, looking happier and more confident, my friend came to me to ask yet again about her marriage. Unfortunately, the cards that came up in her reading prominently were The Devil, Nine of Swords, Judgement reversed and The Tower. These were ominous cards, indicating a negative relationship that would lead to pain, wrong judgement, betrayal and heartache. There was a man in her spread. I asked her if she was in a relationship but she denied it instantly.

Some months later, a common friend told me that she had seen her with a man. Later, I asked my young friend, who confessed to having a love affair with a man many years older than her. She was evasive about the details, but said that she was confident that he was the right man for her and they would get married. Time went by—months became years and the years multiplied, but that man did not marry her. Every time she broached the subject of marriage, he came up with an excuse—his father was ill or he was not earning too well or he wanted to buy a house and so on and so forth. The excuses came glibly and he seemed so sincere and apologetic to her. Yet, when we read the cards, The Devil kept appearing. I gently warned her about the man, but she did not like my advice and instead, got more involved in the relationship. Slowly, she stopped visiting me. Later I learnt that the man did not marry her and after seven long and wasted years, she had begun yet another search for a suitable husband.

I hope and pray that she has found a decent man—she deserves to.

14. Hell or High Water

The phone rang one morning—it was a film star's secretary. She asked if I could come to his residence to do a reading for him. I politely explained that I never did any consultations outside my home and that he was welcome to visit me. Mr X arrived late in the evening, trying to look as inconspicuous as possible. I quickly whisked him away to my consulting room, away from the prying eyes of my staff. In the privacy of the room I assured him of total confidentiality. He was visibly anxious so we did some breathing exercises and once he had relaxed, we started the session.

His problem was that he was in love with two women at the same time. He was able to juggle his relationships, but now things were getting difficult. He was unable to decide which of them was the right person for him. He genuinely loved them both as they satisfied different aspects of his personality. One fulfilled his emotional needs and the other fulfilled his intellectual side. Both were charming, good-looking and deeply in love with him. He did not want to hurt either of them and did not know what to do. He seemed very sincere and concerned about the mess that his life was in. Both women were demanding and there had been ugly scenes that he did not know how to handle. He was terrified that the press would find out and the scandal would destroy his career and his image.

We did a couple of spreads and the women appeared in quick succession. The Queen of Swords, with a sharp incisive intellect and assertive personality, was the one who satisfied his mind. But she had appeared in the area of problems. The other came up as the Queen of Cups—fair and gentle-looking. But she appeared reversed in the spread, indicating that she would cause him problems as well. It was difficult for me to give him any constructive advice, but I told him that neither of these women would be right for him and that he should tone down his relationships with both of them. I advised him to remain friendly with them, but not to think of a long-term relationship. I told him that with time, both the relationships would fade away. It was difficult for him to accept my advice and we tried several times to find an alternative. At last, he reluctantly said he would give it a try.

In the final spread, another Queen appeared—the Queen of Wands—but she was at a distance. Hesitantly, I told him that there could be another woman entering his life, but only if he created space for her and cleared the way for her by being available and unattached to get her attention. She was hovering and it was unclear whether she would come into his life or not, but she was the right woman for him.

To predict time in Tarot is always difficult, but I felt that it would take six months to a year for her to make her appearance. I asked him to let me know if such a person arrived in his life. I could see that he was a little disappointed but had the grace to thank me profusely.

About a year later, the film star's secretary called. She said that he had gone abroad and had asked her to give me a message. It said, somewhat cryptically, 'You were right. The Queen has arrived. Thanks.' I have not heard from him since. I sincerely hope that he has found the Queen of Wands this time and is not mistaking another short-term relationship for the real one. I have seen him with a girl in magazines. She does have a feel of the Queen of Wands, but one can never tell.

15. Anything is Possible

A friend of mine worked for a multinational company (MNC) that was both powerful and effective in India. Though my friend was high up on the corporate ladder, the top post at the MNC was always reserved for a foreigner. Even well-qualified Indians were not given this top post, which came with huge perks and a very handsome salary. The senior staff stagnated and after reaching a certain level, most were compelled to leave the company. My friend was reluctant to go for this option because she liked her work. Due to the downturn in the world economy and the consequent reduction of staff, my friend's employers decided to appoint a local head in one of the regional offices in India. This was a major step and would entail major changes in the way the company functioned. It also meant a huge breakthrough for the local staff. My friend was well positioned for the job, but she was beset with personal problems. She was the sole bread-winner of her family and carried the responsibility of her parental family as well. There were deaths and illnesses in her family that caused havoc in her life, but she braved all these storms, carrying out her responsibilities and going beyond the call of duty. You can imagine the strain that all this caused, not only to her person but to her purse as well. She needed money to manage two homes. She was a fighter but she was getting weary and needed a change for the better. On several occasions, she seriously thought of moving to another city for better prospects but nothing materialized.

One day we were talking on the phone and she mentioned the opening for the top post. She did not plan to apply as she felt that it was an administrative post and that the local finance head would definitely get it. She did not want to apply and be rejected but I felt that there was no harm in trying. I sought the wisdom of Tarot for her and I got fantastic cards. I got the Ace of Swords and The Sun. The Ace of Swords indicates conquest and victory against odds and The Sun shows success and fulfillment of ambition. The cards indicated that she should apply and that she would be successful in winning the post. She had excellent chances.

I called her up and told her this, but she was reluctant as she was not a great believer in Tarot and felt that it would be a waste of time. Eventually, she agreed to apply more out of her affection for me than her belief in my cards. The last date was around the corner and it meant a tremendous effort to put together all the documents and fill in the complicated form. But she did it.

As it turned out, she was selected over 200 applicants. It was a victory indeed and today, she is one of the most successful directors of the company.

16. Patience Always Pays

A young client of mine consulted me several times about a simple problem. She wanted to marry a boy from a different community, but her Brahmin parents were totally against this. Their approach to the problem was to just ignore what she said and continue to show her eligible young men from their community, hoping that she would agree to marry one of them. My friend would throw a fit every time they brought a proposal to her. There would be arguments, but they would finally prevail upon her to meet the boy. She would agree to this and then later back out, leading to arguments. and her storming out of the house. There would be a sullen silence for a while and then the whole process would repeat itself. She worked for a good organization and she would stay away from home on the pretext of work. Matters slowly deteriorated and she stopped talking to her parents.

She wanted to run away from home and marry her boyfriend, but the cards advised her to wait. She agreed to bide her time against her better judgement, but year after year the answer remained the same—wait it out. She was getting frustrated.

The cards further advised her to change her perspective and stop throwing tantrums even though her parents provoked her. I asked her to speak to her parents calmly and explain her situation to them logically and reasonably. I asked her to tell them that she was not interested in seeing, let alone marrying, another man and that they should not waste their time and compromise their position in society for her. If they did not want her to marry the man of her choice, she would not do so, but she should be allowed to live peacefully in the house.

She changed her attitude and instead of being a sullen, constantly abrasive, rebellious daughter, she became reasonable and cooperative. She started going out with her parents, attending other family gatherings and re-establishing their bond. This approach mellowed their attitude and there was peace in their home.

The cards had warned her not to marry without parental consent and to wait for the right time. I must say that she was sorely tried and anyone in her position might have cracked. But she persevered. In the meanwhile, she won a scholarship and travelled abroad for a few months. She left the organization she was working for and we lost touch. Then one day, she phoned to say that at last her parents had agreed to let her marry her boyfriend.

With a few years of patience, she was able to avoid a lifetime of estrangement from her parents and could now live a happy life, free of the guilt she would have felt if she had married against her parents' wishes.

17. The Book that Brought Money

Many years ago, I used to write a column for *Femina* called 'Futurewise', in a question-and-answer format. Readers wrote in with their queries and I would endeavour to give them answers. It was a popular column and *Femina* used to receive a large number of letters from its readers. I kept answering but there was no feedback mechanism so I did not know how much my answers helped people. I also didn't really remember what advice I gave as there were many queries and no way of keeping track.

I had another life, where I worked for a diplomatic organization involved deeply in the arts, literature and other creative areas. I managed a large portfolio of activities for them and one of the aspects of the job was organizing arts and literature events. At one of these events, a lady walked up to me and said that she needed to thank me. I was perplexed and surprised. I had never seen her before and could not figure out what she was thanking me for.

She explained that she had written to me through *Femina* and had received an answer that had worked out as predicted. She was an aspiring novelist and had written a manuscript that she had wanted to get published. She had gone to several publishers but none of them had shown any interest in her work and she had given up hope of ever finding a publisher. Her question had been whether her novel would ever see the light of day.

My answer, as she told me, was that there would be two new publishers but she would have trouble working with them. The contract could get cancelled or they would go back on their word. The result would be a disappointment, followed by delays and postponements. It would be a hard climb but she should not give up. There would be a third publisher and she should wait for him. If she persisted long enough, her novel would get published. Not only that, she would also make a good amount of money from the book.

She kept searching for publishers—as predicted, two publishers came and went, giving her high hopes and then letting her down. She kept trying although the future looked very bleak. The only thing that kept her going was the positive response that she had received from me. She persisted in her efforts and finally, the breakthrough did come, even though it took three long years. Her novel was published and earned her a fair amount of money. She was writing her second novel and had a copy of her book with her which she gave me.

This was the first time that I had received a feedback from the readers of the *Femina* column and it was very heartening. It was a confirmation of what I always believed—that for intuition to operate when reading the cards, one needed just a connection, a date of birth and a name. Sometimes intuition operated brilliantly and sometimes it did not. It all depended on several factors, not the least being the focus and neutrality that you could bring to bear upon your reading. It gave me confidence that I was not working in the dark, that somewhere, I was getting it right. Subsequently, I did receive a number of responses, especially from readers of a similar column that I did until recently for the *Mumbai Mirror*. I still have the copy of the novel that was gifted to me.

18. US, Here I Come...

A good-looking man once came to me for a reading. He was a Punjabi Brahmin and had served in the air force. He had taken an early retirement and wanted to know what he should do in the future. He was unmarried and did not have a great deal of money but he wanted to find a way to make his life successful. He was bright and open-minded and listened carefully to what I said.

His elder brother had started a company in Mumbai and had asked him to join it. He got along well with his sister-in-law and loved his nephew. His youngest brother was also in Mumbai so this seemed to be the best course to take.

We did a spread for him and it turned out that, although working with his brother was a good option, there was a better opportunity for him. But I could not figure out what this was. I asked him if he had other ideas. He said that he had not thought of anything else and could not understand what the cards were trying to tell him.

We started by discussing all the ideas that he might have in his mind and one by one we explored them through the cards. One idea was to leave Mumbai and go to Delhi to try his luck there, but this did not seem a good option at all. Another idea he had was to go back to his home town, live with his parents and find something there, but that, too, was not a workable choice as in the long run, he would get frustrated and would not be able to earn enough.

There was another idea in his mind, which was rather far-fetched as he neither had the resources nor the contacts. It was to go to the US and work there. We did a spread for this and came up with very positive cards like The Sun and the Ace of Cups. I told him that it would be best for him to go to the US and that he would get success there. Not only would his life unfold in an unexpected way but he would find all that he was seeking in the US. He thought for a while, then remembered that he had a friend there who could help him. It was a long shot but he was willing to try. With the friend's help, he found a job. So my friend went off to the US. Not only that, he married an Indian girl whom he found through the matrimonial column of an Indian newspaper. She is a US citizen and my friend is now happily settled in the US, with his life completely transformed.

19. Caught Between Two Women

A beautiful elderly woman came to see me. She looked so lovely that I wondered what she must have looked like when she was younger—she must have been breathtaking. She was very well dressed with diamonds twinkling in her ears. She looked gracious, kind and gentle. She actually lived in another town but frequently visited Mumbai. She gently told me that she had come to consult the cards about her son, showed me his photograph and said that he was in trouble. She began by saying that she knew that he was in the wrong but she wanted a solution for him.

Usually, I don't like to do a reading for a person who is not present. The reason for this is that I don't think it is right to look into another person's life without their knowledge and I worry about the intentions of the questioner and the relationship they might have with the subject of the reading. But the lady's transparent goodness and her genuine concern convinced me to make an exception. Since she was so hesitant to explain the problem, I guessed that it was to do with an extramarital affair. When I asked her, she nodded her head. Her son was about sixty years old. From the photograph, one could tell that he must have been a good-looking man in his younger days, but now he looked bloated, with lines of reckless living on his face. He had a very unsatisfactory relationship with his wife, who was unable to match his sexual ardour, yet he was totally dependent on her. She was the dominant partner in the marriage. Since they lived in a conservative joint family, matters were brushed under the carpet and the wife somehow coped with the situation though she despised him for his needs. He became the head of a powerful organization and that was when the trouble started. He got easy access to women and started having many affairs. The wife encouraged him, turning a blind eye to his sexual liaisons. As long as her supremacy and position was not affected, she accepted his infidelity—but then he got attached to a woman. She was bold and sensual, a complete contrast to his wife, who was hard-hearted, frustrated and cold. The woman matched his ardour and his sexual needs. He could not do without her and the relationship continued for many years. Slowly, she realized her hold over him and demanded marriage, threatening to terminate their relationship if he did not get a divorce. The man was caught between the devil and the deep sea—he could not give up his wife because he was still very dependent on her emotionally. She was tough and managed the politics of his position and his family. The other woman gave him pure pleasure. She satisfied him and after years of denial and one-night stands, he was sexually dependent on her. Both women reacted to the situation—the wife walked out and the mistress threatened to marry another man. So what was he to do? Should he marry the mistress and divorce his wife? Or try to get back his wife and forget the mistress? Both were tough women, who caused him pain and anguish. Both were threatening him and both were capable of leaving him, but he wanted both—he wanted his wife to accept the mistress.

I wondered how such a decent woman could produce such a son. It was probably the karma of her past life that was bearing fruit. Despite his behaviour, it was evident that she loved him and wanted him to be happy. He had no friends, no family and except for his mother, no one was really interested in him. The spreads indicated that neither of the women loved him nor did he love them. Love did not come into the picture. He was a weak man who was used to getting what he wanted. The solution to the problem was that he had to change—he had to leave both of them and start life afresh. Even as I told the mother this, I knew that he would not even try to change. He had appeared as the King of Cups reversed, a double-dealing man who took people for granted. The mistress seemed to be the worst choice for him and though the wife would be cruel to him, she was the better bet. The mistress would leave him in any case, even if he married her. Given the circumstances, going back to his wife was the only viable option.

My suggestion was to try and get the wife back on whatever terms she insisted on. She was not going to make him happy but he would get back a family of sorts. I also told the lady that she should not depend on her son as he would let her down. She found this difficult to believe and was convinced that after this lesson, he would turn over a new leaf.

She thanked me very graciously. I wished I could have said more positive things to her. She had other children but she doted on her son. I asked her to let me know how the situation unravelled itself and she promised me that she would. True to her word, I received a call from her and she told me her son and his wife were together again. The old lady had moved to Mumbai to live with her other children as the son's wife had refused to take care of her and the son, selfish as he was, did nothing to help his mother.

20. A Politician's Son

When a well-known politician's son, a good-looking boy with surprisingly innocent eyes, came to meet me, I recognized him instantly as he looked so much like his father, who was prominently visible on television and in the newspapers. His father was a powerful and successful politician at the national level who had succeeded with a lot of effort and grit. He had the full support of his wife, who stood by him like a rock. For the family, all through their lives, the father's politics had come first. They had all made the necessary sacrifices—changed schools, cities, lifestyles, friends and clothes to suit their father's political situation. The father had come close to going to prison and they had lived with that. When his party had lost, they had nothing to fall back on, but they had gone on. The ups and down and the constant readjustment had taken its toll, but they became a consolidated political family and had established themselves right on the top.

The father was a respectable politician by today's standards. He was loyal and intelligent, soft-spoken and educated. Now he was getting old. He could no longer put in the kind of effort that was required to hold on to political power. He wanted his eldest son, my friend, to be groomed to take his place. His father and mother felt that being the eldest son, it was my friend's duty to step into his father's shoes and carry on the family name. The elections were around the corner. The father proposed that the son contest the elections at the state level to make an entry into politics and slowly work his way up with his support. The father could get him a party ticket to contest the election. He felt that this was a golden opportunity as the party was looking for fresh faces and no one would deny him this favour.

My friend loved his parents, but he felt that he could not commit himself to politics. He was afraid. He did not want to live like his father had. He did not like the world of politics with its manipulations, the constant threat of treachery, the fear, anxiety and stress. For him it was like riding a tiger. He wanted none of it, but he did not want to disappoint or hurt his parents and he knew that he would do both if he did not fall in line with their wishes. He had not even been able to express his views. His parents had taken it as a *fait accompli* that he would join politics and could not imagine anyone saying no to such a great opportunity and honour. His father already had plans well laid out and had started introducing him to key people. My friend felt that he was doomed. He was fully cognizant of the fact that he owed a great deal to his father and that his life had been easy and luxurious because of him. He was torn between his filial duty to his parents, and his own ideas about the kind of life he wanted to live.

He wanted to resolve this situation without causing any grief to his parents. His dream was to move away from the power centre of Delhi to a place like Bangalore, where he could live sanely and quietly with his parents' blessings. What was he to do? How could he get out of this tight situation? Would he be able to manage his parents and live the life that he wanted? He was on the brink of confessing all to his parents, taking their wrath and facing whatever would happen.

We did a few spreads. The first answer that came up was that he should not have a confrontation with his parents, nor tell them to their faces that he would not join politics. The Page of Swords indicated the use of tact and diplomacy as the best course. Six of Swords reversed advised delaying tactics, not to say anything outright but to play a waiting game. The next thing advice was to explore the idea informally with close relatives and see who else might be an appropriate candidate, someone eager to don his father's mantle. The Knight of Swords was prominently positioned—this indicated that there was someone already interested in getting the role. He could not guess who it was as his younger brother was in the US and had no intention of coming back.

Another instruction was that he should go right ahead and buy the property he wanted in Bangalore. The indication was that he would be able to work out his dreams and that he should not worry. There was a family wedding coming up and we decided that he would try to explore possibilities then. There were just a couple of months left for the elections and his father was expected to make the announcement soon. He was worried that once he agreed to his father's wishes, there would be no turning back. No one would let him and all would be over for him.

The cards had indicated that the problem would be worked out. The important thing was to zero in on the right person whom his father would approve of. He looked uncertain but agreed to follow the plan. The family wedding came and went but my friend could not find any such person. The tension mounted as the day for nominations came closer. I was also affected by all that was going on and all that my friend told me on the phone.

Where was the Knight of Swords that could take my friend's place? About a month before the announcement, the father brought home a young person who was a distant relative.The father was impressed by him and felt that he would be able to help my friend. That was our clue. I asked my friend to take this person into his confidence and share his problem with him. It was a risk but the cards indicated that he could be trusted. It turned out that this relative was interested in politics, so my friend was able to indicate his lack of interest in politics to his parents, but also add that the cousin would be the right person to take the father's place. There was disbelief, anger, disappointment, arguments, sulking and some amount of blackmail but finally, acceptance. The plan, as indicated by the cards, had worked and my friend was free to pursue his dreams.

21. A Curse or a Blessing

Two good-looking sisters, very similar to each other, came to see me. Cultured and sophisticated, they belonged to an eminent family. They seemed very subdued, almost in tears, as they narrated the story of their father for whom they had come to seek guidance.

Their father was a well-known business tycoon who had lived an exemplary life of discipline and old-world values. He retired, handed over his huge empire to his son and looked forward to living in peace with his wife whom he adored.

Then one day he had a headache and the next morning, suffered a brain haemorrhage. He was flown into Mumbai and operated on. The prognosis was dire, with the doctors giving him almost no chance of survival. He slipped into a coma and the family kept a twenty-four-hour vigil outside the ICU of the hospital. He was a patriarch on whom many people depended, so many relatives gathered and waited for him to regain consciousness. For all of them, it was like sitting on a volcano. Every day dawned with new hope and ended with a fresh anxiety. Would he survive? What would the damages be? Would he be able to see, hear and talk? How would his vital functions be affected? These questions had no answers since the doctors could not give them an opinion until the patient gained consciousness. The days became weeks, but he remained in a coma. The girls wanted to know what was going to happen to him.

They began to cry openly, saying that their father was a fighter and had survived many problems that had seemed insurmountable. Would he survive this crisis too?

They were also very worried about their mother, who was a delicate woman and dependent on her powerful husband for everything. Emotionally, she was very vulnerable and they were concerned about her health in all this stress and tension. First of, all we did a spread for their father's health and recovery. The cards indicated that he would survive and regain consciousness within a short time. But a very prominent Five of Cups indicated a not-so-happy state of affairs. The image of this card shows five cups, two standing straight and the other three lying with the contents spilled. This indicates that a lot will be taken away but still something will remain intact—though he would survive, his health would be seriously impaired and there would be a major handicap that would compromise his lifestyle. Exploring further, the presence of many Sword cards showed that the area of impact could be primarily the mind, although other parts of the body could not be ruled out. Regarding the mother, there was nothing to fear. She was much stronger than they thought her to be and a prominent Ace of Swords indicated victory and strength.

The patriarch did come out of the coma as indicated but was seriously handicapped. His left side was paralysed and his speech affected. But the most painful outcome was that his mind was seriously impaired. To everyone's surprise the mother emerged the strongest of all and took charge. With the help of her family doctor, she got a couple of nurses, created a hospital room at home, got specialists organized and started to look after him with the same devotion that she had given to him when he was well. When I last heard from the sisters, he was doing well, but the mother had come into her own and was looking after not only her husband but also the huge family business. She was advising her sons and keeping an eye on what was going on, showing a strength of character that no one in the family thought she had.

22. The Advice That Did Not Work

One of the most memorable failures that I have had was an incident related to the health of a close friend's relative.

One day, my friend called to say that her sister-in-law had been admitted to the hospital with a severe stomach ache and that the doctors were unable to diagnose the cause. They tried every possible treatment, but her pain grew and her condition rapidly deteriorated. The family was distraught and did not know what to do.

My friend came for a reading to ask whether her sister-in-law would be cured or not. Would she recover and get back to her normal happy life? The spread indicated some health issues with the card of the Nine of Wands reversed. That the sickness was unexpected was indicated by the Page of Swords reversed and her suffering was suggested by the Ten of Swords. In the result position, I had the card of the World and at a distance there was the card of the Empress. To me, this was an indication of freedom from pain and the enjoyment of life. I told my friend so and she went back reassured.

But then there was bad news—within a couple of days, the sister-in-law passed away without the doctors finding out what had happened to her. I was taken aback. I could not understand where I had gone wrong in my prediction. After checking my logbook, I realized that I had interpreted the cards wrongly. The card of the World in the result position indicated freedom from pain but not by getting well—it meant succumbing to the illness instead. The World also stood for freedom from this life while the Empress indicated the afterlife abundance of the soul. Tarot does not talk about death as it is all about living, but in this case, I did not pick up the right signal. I suppose I wanted to be the harbinger of good news.

I hope these stories showed you a little of how Tarot works. There is one word of advice that I would like to leave you with. The truths and guidance of new age sciences and Tarot are pointers and indicators to help you as you tread the path of life and make it a little easier for you to take the right decisions. They are not necessarily gospel truths to be followed blindly. Remember that you have a free will and you need to take decisions consciously, bearing full responsibility for your actions. It is not advisable to depend completely on any esoteric science for all decisions, as this would cripple your will, understanding and your growth process. Seek help, but let it connect with your inner resources and be revalued and processed through your inner lens. In this way, you will understand yourself better and your decision will have the force and the strength of your being, leading to inner richness, development and growth as well.

Chapter Four

Correspondences:

Tarot and Other Esoteric Sciences.

4.

Tarot and Other Esoteric Sciences: Correspondences

I have been fascinated by various new age sciences that focus on the evolution of humanity to a higher consciousness. I have read about the runes and *I Ching*, the Chinese classic text also known as the *Book of Changes*. I have heard so much about Kabbalah, the Jewish mystical school of thought, and read about sun signs, *chakra*s and planetary influences and wondered whether all these esoteric sciences and mystic schools of thought have any connections. It has been a journey of discovery as I gradually realized that although each esoteric science is garbed in different languages, symbols and perspectives, they have a common ground and deep connections. New age sciences look at universal laws and help us to understand how to apply them to improve the human lot. Their aim is to help us live better lives by teaching us how to know ourselves better and to heal aspects of the self that are causing problems and pain. Through meditation, they help us connect to the source of our being. They are meant for spiritual growth and guidance, to show us where we are going wrong and how to make changes in our perspective that will bring about positive change in our lives. They also help us to understand future trends and suggest ways of managing these, giving startling insights.

The human race has faced the same issues and predicaments throughout human history. We forget our true calling and live in a way that is not in harmony with the natural laws of existence, causing us to suffer. Shamans and other spiritual masters have gained knowledge through turning inwards and connecting with the inner being. They have come up with signs, symbols, numbers, images and lines through which they try to express and interpret the universe and its laws.

I Ching consists of aphorisms and advice regarding the problems of life, which are represented by sixty-four hexagrams, each with six lines that distill the essence of a particular situation and suggest an appropriate response. The meaning and suggestions of the hexagrams have some strong similarities with other esoteric sciences. *I Ching* is based on an acceptance of change, based on the theory of yin and yang or the opposites in existence. Once we understand the eternal laws, that life is about reconciling opposites and flowing with the Tao (or non-resistence to the challenges that come up in life), we can change our lives. Lao-tse's philosophy teaches that and *I Ching* interprets it. It is not merely a book of divination but of wisdom, philosophy and guidance.

Runes are symbols that were used in northern Europe from the first century AD and evolved into alphabets later. Each symbol has a specific meaning. In Scandinavia, runes are sacred signs engraved on natural oak bark that are used to discover the will of heaven and the most likely outcome of the questions posed to the oracle. Rune binds (two or more runes written together) and rune scripts can influence the course of events.

Kabbalah is about the twenty-two secret pathways to God corresponding with the twenty-two cards of the Major Arcana in Tarot, which are universal laws in operation and archetypal energies at play.

Numerology with its basic numbers of 1–9, the twelve sun signs and the nine planets, all have interesting similarities and connections. Each number has a core value and indicates a certain perspective, which impacts a person who has that number prominent in his name, date of birth and so on. Numbers indicate your temperament and possibilities in your life. Aligning with the cosmic laws allows you to flow and live in greater harmony. It allows you to take advantage of opportunities and avoid pitfalls.

Chakras are energy nodes situated on the spinal cord that distribute psychic and physical energy to the body. The correct movement or spinning of the *chakras* brings health and healing. If they have blocks, this can cause problems.

Esoteric sciences emerge from a common need and connect with each other. It must be noted though that these correspondences are not written in stone. They are only starting points to help you widen your understanding and build connections with other esoteric sciences. You might see them differently, which is just fine. I have taken my ideas from different sources like the Golden Dawn occult concepts filtered down into the books of modern Tarot masters, as well as Indian concepts of *chakra*s and healing with gemstones. I have modified these based on my thoughts and experience. I have, for some time now, also dabbled in *I Ching*, runes and numerology, and have presented my current thoughts in this chapter. They are open to being challenged and modified.

Though we do not know the exact origins of Tarot, it can be seen that the oracle draws from many different kinds of esoteric sciences, including astrology, numerology and Kabbalah. It uses colours, symbols, magic, alchemy, spirituality, psychology, religion and mythology and has correspondences with runes, *I Ching*, *chakra*s and oriental thought. Strong elements of Christian references are also a part of Tarot traditions.

One of the theories about the origin of Tarot, as mentioned earlier in this book, is that it was created in an esoteric conference in the city of Fez where masters and practitioners of different esoteric disciplines put together the Tarot cards as a secret method of communication and spiritual evolution. Hence the various esoteric sciences have some correspondence with Tarot and seem to have contributed in developing the Tarot cards. To understand Tarot, it is also important to know about the influences and correspondences in order to expand the depth of your understanding and connection with the cards.

Numerology and Tarot

Numerology is the study of numbers and the impact that they have on our lives. The science of numerology is considered much older than Tarot. In the West, numerology goes back to the philosophy of Pythagoras, the Greek thinker, who believed that the universe is made of mathematical patterns and all parts and aspects of it can be expressed in numbers that correspond to universal vibrations. Therefore, all things, including names, words, birth dates and birthplaces can be reduced to numbers in order to determine the personalities, destinies, inclinations and fortunes of individuals. Odd numbers are usually regarded as forceful, yang or masculine while even numbers are considered stabilizing, yin or feminine. It is believed that numbers were invented by the Arabs, but the source of their knowledge was the Hindus who, in turn, were given their knowledge by the gods.

The numbers and the images of Tarot correspond and connect with each other and numerology adds to the interpretation of Tarot. The qualities and attributes of the numbers and the images of Tarot are closely connected. This has a significance because understanding the number associated with a card helps you to experience the meaning and the energy of the card better.

The primary numbers are 1–9 while 10–22 are compound numbers, which can be reduced to primary numbers and be influenced by both the numbers that make up the compound number. For example, the number twenty-one has the power of numbers two and one as well as a strong connection with three, which is the reduced primary number. These connections add different shades to the final meaning of the card.

Given below are meanings of numbers and their correspondences with the Major Arcana in Tarot:

Primary numbers

0 Zero is the number of pure potential, of absolute beginnings and endings and a return to nothingness. The Fool in the Major Arcana bears this number and is conceived of as the soul before it comes into manifestation and is about to begin the journey of life. It is in the potential stage and its power is still to be realized.

I Number one is the number of individuality, aggression, force and creativity. It is the beginning of an idea, an action and a venture. The number one contains raw energy and power. As it is still not fully channelled energy, it can go wrong. The Magician carries number I. He is the power of the conscious mind, the will, the energy that brings ideas into manifestation, the vibrant energy that can get what it wants by magic or trickery. There can be rashness in both.

II Two is the number of duality, balance and passivity. There is compromise in number two, which does not appear in number one. It is a gentle number. Number II in Tarot is represented by The High Priestess who sits between two pillars, which are black and white, indicating balance and representing the power of the subconscious mind, passive acceptance, and the coupling that is to come.

III Three is the number of unity, of completion, abundance and creativity. In numerology, number three is concerned with a person's ability to live life. It is a powerful number and in Tarot, is depicted by The Empress, the mother goddess of plenty who is constantly pregnant and who represents growth, luxury, abundance and creativity.

IV Four is the number of manifestation and material reality. There are four elements, four sides of a square, four cardinal directions, four seasons, and so on. It is a number of order, structure and earthly power. Number IV is represented in Tarot by The Emperor who is the lord of stability, power, responsibility and earthly dominion.

V Five is a number related to the five human senses and can represent a crisis of the senses or a state of instability. Freedom is a concern of this number. In Tarot, it is represented by The Hierophant who is a teacher and leader. The card is also known as The Pope, standing for calmness and serenity. The Pope can control a crisis by the power of religion and strong traditions that can reduce the havoc of the senses.

VI Six represents the adjustments and cooperation required for the harmony that returns when we resolve the disruption and instability seen in the number five This is a new equilibrium and is represented by the card of The Lovers, which indicates pleasure and a relationship with the another person, leading to harmony after making a choice.

VII Seven has been held as a magical number—there are seven colours in a rainbow and the world was created in seven days. This number holds spiritual significance. Number seven explores our inner capabilities. It also signifies victory and conquest. It is an active, forceful number. In the Major Arcana, The Chariot corresponds to this number. The card is related to triumph, victory and progress—The Charioteer is the supreme conqueror of the self and his confidence is based on his successful self-relization.

VIII This number is about endurance and strength and it seeks spiritual harmony. It is represented in Tarot by the card of Strength, of taming the wild beast within all of us. It is a number of faith, acceptance and single-mindedness. It is ruled by Saturn. It brings obstacles but rewards us at the end. People associated with the number eight will need to learn spiritual lessons in life, sometimes painfully.

IX Nine is the last single digit in the series of 1–9. It carries connotations of the completion of a cycle. It can signify the wisdom that is achieved toward the end of a cycle. In Tarot, number nine is represented by the Hermit, the wise one who is ready to help others and give selfless advice.

Compound numbers

X In number ten we see the final ending. Number ten is the essence of change and lucky breaks, but also of uncertainty. One cycle has ended and a new one is beginning. In Tarot, The Wheel of Fortune represents the uncertainty and originality of The Fool, number 0, and the conscious power of The Magician to make things happen. The Wheel of Fortune suggests that even if you have had some lucky breaks, you must keep your balance and continue to develop.

XI Number eleven is made up of 1+1=2 and carries the energies of both these numbers. The conscious mind, will and force is balanced by the subconscious, which is passive and receiving, thus creating the true balance for Justice, which is the combination of these seemingly opposing qualities. The right combination is integral to this number, which is considered a master number.

XII This number is made up of 1+2=3. In number twelve, the surrender of number two transforms the aggression of number one and creates an abundance of three in spiritual terms. It means surrendering all that you have to gain the kingdom of heaven—therefore, it is also a number of sacrifice. This is also considered a master number—there are twelve months in a year, twelve apostles of Christ and twelve signs of the zodiac. When this number appears, alertness is required to see the right perspective.

XIII This number is a higher octave of number IV, The Emperor. As history tells us, kings or rulers have often ascended the throne after battles or after the deaths of rivals. This is a number suggesting that if power is unwisely used, it can lead to destruction and death. It is the aggression of number one and the completion of number three that combine in the number XIII, the card of Death.

XIV Number fourteen combines the transmuting energy of number I, The Magician and the wisdom of number IV, The Emperor, with the power of number V, The Hierophant. It has the magical healing powers of The Magician, the knowledge of The Hierophant and the strength and responsibility of The Emperor. In Tarot, number XIV is Temperance, the healing angel.

XV This is the number of our times where the pleasure-seeker and the rebel combine. It uses the wildness and trickery of number I, The Magician, the sexual distortion of number VI, The Lovers and the outward superficiality of number V, The Hierophant to combine in number XV, The Devil.

XVI A destructive and explosive combination of number I, The Magician and the distortion of number VI, The Lovers with the ego and overconfidence of number VII, The Chariot, this number can signify danger. In Tarot, number XVI is represented by The Tower, which is the edifice of ego and is related to destruction.

XVII A higher octave of eight, this number combines beautifully with aspects of the positive will and self-realization of number seven. Associated with harmony, hope and insight, number seventeen also has the potential for healing the mind. In Tarot, this number is represented by The Star, which gives insight and hope

XVIII A number of conflicts with the material and spiritual worlds are depicted by numbers one and eight. A difficult balance can lead to loneliness and imaginary demons. In Tarot, number XVIII is represented by the card of The Moon.

XIX Combining the energies of the success of number one, the wisdom of number nine and the luck of number ten, number nineteen is one of the most powerful numbers, indicating success and victory over ill luck and darkness and the attainment of wisdom and knowledge. The Sun in Tarot is number XIX, and brings light, success and happiness.

XX The subconscious power of number II of The High Priestess combined with the innocence of number 0, The Fool, leads to the resurrection and awakening of a being and opening of the doors of the mind and the subconscious. Number twenty leads to the awakening of some *chakra*s. Judgement is number XX in Tarot.

XXI Combining 2+1=3 in a different order than in The Hanged Man, this number leads to liberation and freedom rather than inaction and suspension. It is a fortunate number, indicating a new beginning is at hand. The power of the subconscious of The High Priestess, the freedom and the energy of The Magician, combined with the abundance and emotional fulfillment of The Empress, is the final liberation of the card of The World in Tarot.

Tarot and Astrology

Concepts of astrology, the characteristics of the nine planets and the twelve signs of the zodiac seem to have considerable correspondence with Tarot. There are similarities and strong resonances between astrology and Tarot and it is interesting to know how they connect. Seeing the cards through the prism of astrology should give the reader an added perspective. People proficient in astrology can relate to this and add another dimension to their interpretation of the cards.

The **sun** or *surya* is the most powerful planet in the sky, with the strongest impact on human destiny. The attributes of the sun are brightness, success, positivity and nurturing qualities, recognition and power. It rules the sun sign of Leo and is the lord of the fifth house, the house of creativity in the astrological chart (most horoscopes are divided into houses, which stand for different spheres of life and are calculated according to the exact date and place of birth). In Tarot, The Sun has similar attributes. The Sun card suggests resolution of problems and the dispelling of darkness.

The **moon** or *chandra* rules the sun sign Cancer and governs the fourth house, the house of the mother in the astrological chart. The moon governs the mind and the emotions. It generates love of beauty, creativity and imagination. In Tarot, The Moon suggests the waxing and waning of emotions, primordial fears and morbid imagination. Only after crossing the towers of The Moon will The Fool reach The Sun on the other side.

Venus or Shukra rules Taurus and Libra. It governs the second and the seventh houses, of wealth and partnerships. It deals with charm and beauty, luxuries and grace. Representing the feminine, Venus is attractive and creative. In Tarot, The Empress is ruled by Venus. She is fertile in her womanhood. She is the mother goddess of plenty. As she sits in the field of ripe corn with a lush green forest all around her, she suggests creativity, grace, warmth and generousity.

Mars or Mangal is a planet of power and energy. It is strong and unbending and is also considered a planet of war. However, it can be a planet of destruction and in Indian astrology, a malefic Mars is believed to cause quarrels and breakups in a marriage. Mars rules Aries and co-rules Scorpio. In Tarot, The Tower has the negative potency of Mars and causes explosions and upheavals that make you look at your ego and your motives. It delivers one of the toughest lessons that the Fool has to learn.

Mercury or Budh moves very fast in the sky and stays in one sign only for a short while. Mercury rules Gemini and also Virgo. Mercury is about communication and intellectual agility. It can be critical, heartless and fussy and gives too much attention to detail. It can gossip, lie and slander. In Tarot, The Magician represents the energy of Mercury. He is quick-witted, capable and stimulating, but he can also be a trickster who uses ploys and deceit to realize his aims.

Jupiter or Guru is the planet of luck, money and abundance as well as the planet of wisdom and education. Jupiter rules Sagittarius and Pisces. The Wheel of Fortune, which represents this planet in Tarot, has the blue sphinx on the top of the wheel, showing that life should be lived with detachment, as an observer. The Wheel of Fortune brings luck, money and surprises.

Saturn or Shani is a planet of judgements and trial and also of reward and resurrection. In Indian astrology, Shani, considered the son of Surya, is one of the most powerful planets. The Judgement in Tarot, which illustrates this theme, is about vindication and reversals, of undoing the past and beginning all over again. Some Tarot traditions believe there is a greater correspondence between Shani and the World card in Tarot. This may be due to the powerful place that Shani enjoys in Indian astrology, but I think Judgement works better.

Neptune is the watery planet that seeks spirituality through sacrifice. It is a powerful planet that is dreamy, unworldly, fluid, sensitive, intuitive and psychic. The Hanged Man represents this planet for he has suspended decisions. He sacrifices himself for the good of the world—he is not about action but about contemplation and surrender.

Uranus is the latest discovery in astrology. It is a planet characterized by impulsiveness, radical change and sudden happenings. This planet has the stamp of a genius and revolutionary and encourages unconventional behaviour. The Fool in Tarot has similar characteristics to Uranus—he too, is risk-taking, adventurous and impulsive. He loves to be an original and dares to go where angels fear to tread, yet he is innocent and trusting. The Order of the Golden Dawn has attributed the card of the World to this planet but the essence of the planet and the card do not seem to match. The card of the World is about liberation not impulse; it is not radical like Uranus.

Pluto is erratic and powerful and destroys outmoded concepts. Pluto is the god of the underworld or rebirth. The card of Death in Tarot relates to this planet for it is as erratic as Pluto and can even bring powerful kings to their knees. The card of Death in Tarot suggests change and new opportunities. The Order of the Golden Dawn suggests the card of Judgement is associated with Pluto, but Judgement is about resurrection and rebirth, rather than death and change.

The other two powerful presences in Indian and in western astrology are Rahu and Ketu, called the north node and the south node, respectively, but I have not found any significant resonance with the Tarot cards.

The Sun Signs and Tarot

Opinions on what sun sign is in harmony with which Tarot card differ and vary. You are free to draw your own conclusions, but I will give reasons explaining why I think a particular card has a greater relevance to a specific sun sign.

ZODIAC SUN SIGNS

Aries/The Fool: Though some Tarotologists ascribe The Emperor to the sign of Aries because of the ram's head on his throne and his daring approach to life, The Emperor is far more stable and responsible than the hot-headed impulsive ram. The Fool fits better in his naivety, impulsiveness and risk-taking approach. Aries also stands for a child-like foolishness that is ascribed to The Fool.

Taurus/ Hierophant/The Emperor: Though broadly speaking, both The Hierophant and The Emperor express some aspects of Taurus, I feel The Emperor expresses the Taurean character better. The Emperor's power, his stubbornness, determination, stability and his ability to go beyond limitations is in line with the Taurus character more than the traditional and socially organized Hierophant.

Gemini/The Lovers: The sun sign Gemini and The Lovers card are both about choice, harmony and communication, even though in Gemini the emphasis is also on intellectual agility and changeability, while The Lovers card emphasizes the relationship aspect and the harmony between people. Romantic love is an important aspect of The Lovers card, which perhaps is not so prominent in the sun sign of Gemini, but both Gemini and The Lovers are ruled by Mercury.

Cancer/The Moon: The sun sign of Cancer is about emotions and imagination. It is also about getting excessively attached and may cause imaginary fears. The card of The Moon features the crab, which is associated with Cancer, or shellfish. The Moon card indicates the path shown by The Tower that one must travel to reach The Sun on the other side. It is about dealing with primordial instincts and fears; about evolution and growth; and also about poetry and beauty. The crab in both the card and the sun sign has to learn to let go. Some scholars think that The Chariot represents the planet of the moon better because of the lunar image on The Charioteer's jacket. The sun sign of Cancer is ruled by the moon.

Leo/Strength: The sun sign Leo is about generosity, courage, energy, passion and a larger-than-life existence. Leos are the kings of the zodiac and need the attention fit for a king. The card of Strength is about taming passions and the fires within us and emerging victorious. It is about having endurance and courage and faith in the divine and controlling desires effortlessly. The image of the lion is a feature common to the sun sign and the card.

Virgo/Hermit: People of the Virgo sun sign are critical of others and excel at what they do because they are hardworking and have an eye for detail. They are usually self-sufficient and unemotional. The card of The Hermit is about giving expert advice. He is alone on the hill-top, guiding travellers who lose their way. The Hermit is about introspection and self-sufficiency. Virgo is ruled by Mercury.

Libra/Justice: Libra is a social, garrulous creature who has a great sense of style and beauty. Justice and fair play are important to Librans and balance—which they seek all their lives—is a need. The card of Justice, too, is about the balance of head and heart. It is about objective understanding and the courage to speak frankly. Justice is a card indicating a preoccupation with right and wrong. Libra is ruled by Venus.

Scorpio/Death/Judgement: The sun sign Scorpio is the only sign of the zodiac that can transform itself completely. It is about explosive intensity, passionate emotions and obsessive ego. It is represented by three creatures: the scorpion, the grey lizard and the eagle. The card of Judgement is about resurrection and total change, leaving behind past traumas and wrongs. It is about judgements and objective decisions and is a vindication of the human spirit. Some Tarotologists feel that the card of Death is more appropriate for the sun sign Scorpio. Scorpio is ruled by Pluto.

Sagittarius/Magician: The fire sign of Sagittarius has the energy to transform things. Sagittarians are people with a capacity to enjoy life, who love travelling, experiencing new things and meeting people, but who sometimes resort to trickery. The Magician can draw energy from above and transform it into manifestations. He has the willpower and the capability to solve all issues. The Magician is the master of all the four suits of Tarot. Like Sagittarians, he is able to get what he wants by devious means. Sagittarius is ruled by Jupiter.

Capricorn/Hierophant: Capricorn, the sure-footed goat, plods on till he reaches the top. No one and nothing can stop him. Careful about the outside world and money, Capricorn is very hardworking and will keep his ideas to himself till he translates them to reality—he rarely lets himself go. The Hierophant is the power of the external religion that controls the outside world with tried and tested methods. He is tradition and received wisdom. He is an educator and operates in a social milieu where money and appearances are important. Capricorn is ruled by Saturn.

Aquarius/The Star: The sun sign Aquarius is forward-looking. People born under this sign are searching for insight into experiences, motives and reasons. They are intelligent and have a tactful way of dealing with people. The Star is a symbol of hope and is also about insight and finding inward motives. The Star is about the future and what is to come rather than the past. Aquarius is ruled by Uranus.

Pisces/The High Priestess: The Pisces sun sign is about emotions and sensitivity, creativity and poetry, imagination and need. In affinity with Pisces, The High Priestess deals with the subconscious mind and has intuitive knowledge—she wears a crown made up of the moons of imagination and emotions. She sits between black and white pillars, signifying choosing between two courses of action (Pisceans are always trying to decide a course of action). Pisces is ruled by Neptune.

Runes and Tarot

The runes are symbols from which the alphabet emerged. They were used as by the ancient Norse people for divinatory readings and magical spells. Norse mythology tells us that the runes were handed down from Odin, the highest god in the Norse hierarchy, to be carved into wood and read. The word 'rune' comes from the word 'runa', which means 'mystery', a term that applies to the present, since everything about the runes remains a mystery.

The most popular set of runes in use today are known as the 'Elder Futhark' and consist of twenty-four symbols or letters. These runes can be a powerful means of communication with the higher realms and contain the knowledge of the universe. They can represent gods, people, objects, animals, concepts and occurrences.

The runes are meant to be carved or burnt into a surface, not written. It is believed that Odin hung from Yggdrasil, the Tree of Life, impaled on his own spear for nine days and nights in order to gain knowledge of the runes. Runes were made only from natural oak as the tree was held in great esteem by the Norse and Celts for its longevity, size and

RUNES

nutritious acorns. The oak is frequently associated with gods of thunder and lightning such as Zeus and Thor. Nowadays, runes are made from various natural materials, such as clay, wood, and gemstones like jade and crystal. Only natural stains from organic matter are used to create the symbols.

Some practitioners of the esoteric sciences believe that runes were the inspiration for Tarot. For instance, it is thought that The Hanged Man in the Tarot is Odin, the Norse god, who hung upside down from the Yggdrasil tree to get knowledge. There are different views regarding the correspondence between these two new age sciences. Though there is no known historical record of any correspondence between Tarot and runes and some scholars believe that there is no real correspondence, other scholars argue that there are many similarities and a definite correspondence. There are varying opinions on Tarot cards and the corresponding runes that express similar ideas and energies. There is no unanimous opinion about the perfect fit, but different perspectives need to be allowed. As both these sciences are esoteric instruments used to explore the human mind and spirit, to learn lessons about life and understand experiences, the universal energies tapped by them will have some correspondence. The shape and the methodology may differ; a Tarot card or a rune may not be exactly like each other but both will explore the same basic questions of human existence and the inner power of the mind.

Some non-controversial correspondences between the twenty-two Major Arcana cards and the twenty-four runes are:

a. The energy of the sun represented in Tarot cards and in runes—in runic terminology, it is called Sigil or Sowele; in Tarot, it is the Sun card.

b. The death rune is Eoh or Eihwaz, while in Tarot, we have the Death card.

c. The Hagalaz or Haegl runes are associated with an explosive force that destroys order, much like The Tower in Tarot.

d. The Lagaz or Lagu runes and The High Priestess in Tarot focus on intuition and the inner being.

Given below is a full correspondence with options.

Tarot–Rune Connections

Rune	Meaning	Tarot Card
Algiz	protection; understanding emotions; antlers of an elk; reaching up to the divine wisdom; vision; clarity of the mind	IX The Hermit
Ansuz	signals; communication and creativity and divine power; knowledge, wisdom; could be a trickster	I The Magician
Berkana	physical and mental growth; purification; renewal; birch twig	V The Hierophant
Dagaz	day after a long night; spiritual divine light; breakthrough; balance of opposites; cyclical nature of life	XVII The Star
Ehwaz	movement; speed; horse; purpose and forward motion; journeys; spiritual advancement	VII The Chariot
Eihwaz	transformation; rune magic; yew tree associated with death	XIII Death
Fehu	possessions or cattle, a measure of wealth to the ancients; associated with abundance; fulfillment; Frey's rune (the Norse god of fertility)	III The Empress
Gebo	partnership; love; marriage; forgiveness; artistic ability; choice	VI The Lovers
Hagalaz	disruption; damaging natural forces; hailstorm in life; limitation; need for radical change	XVI The Tower

Ingwaz	angel; Ing, Norse god of fertility; peace; harmony; love; energy and action	XIV Temperance
Isa	stillness; stagnation; cold; danger; beautiful but treacherous; purity of ice; snow queen	XVIII The Moon
Jera	seasons; harvest; fruition; result of karma; achievement of goal; cycles of rebirth	IX The Wheel of Fortune
Kano	opening; creative impulses; concentration; personal growth; discernment; illumination, fire, inner light; resolving dilemmas; new insight	XX Judgement
Lagus	relates to the moon; tidal waves; flow; water cleansing; psychic ability; changeability; fluidity; creative potential; imagination	XVIII The Moon or II The High Priestess
Mannaz	the self; mankind; soul; awareness; inner being	O The Fool
Nauthiz	constraint; need; compulsion; desire; craving; courage and wisdom for decisions; dietary aberration; need to control emotions; misplaced love; dark, repressed side of a person	XV The Devil
Othila	group order and prosperity; land of birth; spiritual heritage; experience; fundamental values; aid in spiritual and physical journeys	V The Hierophant
Perdhro or Perth	initiation; mystery; unknown outcome; understanding how to react to given circumstances	XII The Hanged Man
Raido	journeys; riding a vehicle; balance; foresight and fortitude	XIV Temperance

Sowelu	wholeness; light energy; warmth; victory; spiritual awareness; strength of character; power and energy of the sun	XIX The Sun
Thyrisaz	gateway; a thorn; resisting temptation; protection; energy that can be used for good or bad; hammer of Thor, god of thunder	XI Justice
Tiewaz	warrior; Tyr, Norse god of war; fearless and courageous; stability; master tactician; consummate diplomat; male sexuality	IV The Emperor
Uruz	strength; wild ox; endurance and courage; male potency; good health	VIII Strength or The Chariot
Wunjo	joy and hope; ambitions fulfilled; new beginning; discovery of the truth; reward and satisfaction	XXI The World

Other options:
Raido: X Wheel of Fortune
Kano: II High Priestess or VII The Chariot
Wunjo: VIII Strength and O The Fool
Nauthiz: XI Justice

Chakras and Tarot

Just as there are circulatory, respiratory, skeletal, digestive, glandular, nervous and sensory systems in the human body, Indian spiritual systems and Ayurveda recognize that there is also an energy system which spreads energy or *prana* throughout the physical and subtle body. This is closely linked with your physical, emotional and spiritual well-being.

There are three *nadi*s or energy channels in the body. These are called:

The Ida *nadi*, which is located on the left of the spinal column and is the feminine channel.

The Pingila *nadi*, which is located on the right of the spinal column and is the male channel.

The Sushumna *nadi*, which is located along the spinal column in the centre of the body.

Fine networks of energy channels spread all over the body from these *nadi*s, which are parallel to the spinal column.

The seven main *chakra*s are located on the Sushumna *nadi*. They begin from the base of the spine to the top of the head, along the major nerve junctions or ganglia. The word *chakra* comes from Sanskrit and means 'a spinning wheel'. These *chakra*s are nodes of spiritual energy in motion, which receive, transform and distribute energy or *prana* throughout the physical and subtle body. They draw *prana* from all manifestations and transform it into energy that is required by the body for sustenance and growth. This energy connects with the environment and the cosmos.

Each chakra is shaped like a lotus flower and each has a different number of petals, depending on the number of energy channels in the *chakra* through which the energy can flow. *Chakra*s, the energy centres, operate through vibration, light, sound and colour and are impacted by them. For spiritual advancement and emotional and physical well-being, it is important that these *chakra*s are spinning and vibrating in balance because their imbalance is the cause of all human problems.

The Kundalini arises from the base of the Sushumna *nadi*. This is the serpent energy, which is coiled at the lower end of the spine—it is also called Shakti or female divine energy. The Ida *nadi* on the left carries the feminine, cool lunar energy while the Pingla *nadi* on the right carries the male, solar, hot energy. Both these *nadi*s and the Sushumna join together at the Agya *chakra*, the meeting point of all the three *nadis*.

Ayurveda, the traditional system of Indian medicine, used the *chakra* system as early as 2500 BC for holistic healing as the proper functioning of the *chakra*s leads to the full development of a personality—materially, physically and spiritually. Tarot energy can be used to activate and stimulate these *chakra*s by focusing the appropriate energy of a specific Tarot card into the right *chakra*s. (See chapter five for the exercise given for meditation by using Tarot energy).

The first *chakra*: The Mooladhar or root *chakra* is located at the base or the tail-end of the spine. This *chakra* is the foundation of our physical body and survival instincts. It connects us to the physical world, stimulates vital forces and keeps us grounded. It influences the immune system, the capacity for endurance, the fight or flight response and

CHAKRAS

issues of food, clothing and shelter. It is connected with the collective consciousness. Relationships and experiences in early life influence this *chakra*. If it is damaged, issues relating to achievement and strength of character can come up and it could result in an inability to complete what is started, a lack of endurance and fear for safety. Lack of stability and trust are also connected with this *chakra*. Where relationships are concerned, issues with the father are connected to this *chakra* as the father is the foundation of our personalities. To balance this *chakra*, it is vital to connect with the earth. Sit on the ground in a lotus position and walk barefoot on earth—doing activities that connect you to the earth will have a positive impact on this *chakra*. Meditating on the Mooladhar chakra will help to clear any blockages in it.

Colour: fiery red.
Element: earth
Shape: a lotus flower with four petals
Sense: smell
Sound: LAM
Musical note: SA
Aroma oil: clove or cedar oil. Apply it on the *chakra*.
Crystal: carnelian, agate, or blood stone

Tarot correspondence: Tarot Key number O: The Fool
Focus the energy of this card on the Mooladhar *chakra* to activate it.

The second *chakra*: The Swadhisthan or spleen *chakra* is located about two inches below the navel and is connected to our sexual and reproductive capacities. It is the basis of our relationship with the opposite sex. Our ability to feel emotions and sensations is connected with this *chakra*. The sense of taste and the pleasures of life are located here. Sexual love, open-mindedness and the ability work in harmony are all associated with this *chakra*. It also governs the organs of the lower abdomen.

If this *chakra* is working well, a person is open, friendly, imaginative and creative and it helps the person learn from experiences. In personal associations, this *chakra* affects the relationship with the mother. Problems in this *chakra* lead to rejection of sexuality, sexual guilt and emotional problems. There could be excessiveness in the area of food, drugs and sex, a yearning for fulfilling sexual union and problems of the reproductive organs.

The moon helps in healing this *chakra*. Lie down under the full moon and allows the rays to penetrate you. *Sharad Purnima*, (a special full moon night) is an important day to heal this *chakra*, when eating special food infused with the moonlight is effective. Learning to let go, to loosen up physically, can help in balancing this *chakra*.

Colour: orange
Element: water
Shape: A lotus flower of six petals
Sense: taste
Musical note: RE
Sound: VAM
Aroma oil: apply ylang-ylang or sandalwood on the *chakra* to activate it.
Crystal: carnelian or coral

Tarot correspondence: Tarot Key number III: The Empress.
Focus the energy of The Empress on this *chakra*.

The third *chakra*: The Manipur or solar plexus *chakra* represents the centre of our personal universe, the sun. The chakra is located two inches above the navel. It is the seat of our identity, of self-power, self-acceptance and self-worth. It is connected with the astral body and out-of-the-body experiences. Digestion and the organs of the abdomen are governed by it. If this *chakra* works well, it makes a person well adjusted and successful, giving a feeling of safety, security and discipline. The ability to deal with change is the result of the smooth functioning of this *chakra*.

Blocks in this *chakra* lead to anger, lack of self-worth, feelings of rejection, digestive problems, problems with authority, and an inability to manage situations or people. The sun helps in healing this *chakra*—focus on the golden light of the sun, fields of ripe golden corn and yellow sunflowers to heal it.

Colour: yellow
Element: fire
Shape: A lotus with ten petals
Sense: sight

Musical note: GA
Sound: RAM
Aroma oil: lavender or cinnamon. Use the oil on the *chakra* to stimulate it.
Crystal: cetrine, amber and golden topaz

Tarot correspondence: Tarot Key number XIX: The Sun
Draw the energies from The Sun card and focus it on this *chakra*.

The fourth *chakra*: The Anahata or the heart *chakra* is the centre of the *chakra* system. It connects the three lower *chakra*s, which deal with personal consciousness, to the three higher *chakra*s of universal consciousness. All six *chakra*s converge to the Anahata *chakra* which is the meeting point of our spiritual and personal energies. It is focused on love, compassion, forgiveness, empathy, trust and equilibrium. It influences the lungs and the endocrine system.

A well balanced Anahata *chakra* leads to acceptance, unconditional love and a strong connection with nature—it makes us help people. It keeps a person in balance, and gives generosity and prosperity. Problems in this *chakra* impact the immune system, heart and the lungs. There is a lack of compassion and balance, a feeling of instability and of being unloved. Communication with nature in all its forms, music, and poetry help activate this *chakra*. A quiet walk down unspoiled, green countryside helps in healing this *chakra*. Giving to others also heals it.

Colour: green and pink
Element: air
Shape: a lotus with twelve petals
Sense: touch
Musical note: MA
Sound: YAM
Aroma oil: rose. Apply it on the *chakra*.
Crystal: emerald, jade, rose quartz and ruby

Tarot correspondence: Tarot Key number XIV: Temperance.
Focus on the energy of the card and direct it to the *chakra*.

The fifth *chakra*: The *Vishuddhi* or throat *chakra* is tied to communication, good judgement, truthfulness and clairaudience. It impacts the mouth, throat, teeth and thyroid gland. Cognitive abilities and sound are connected with this *chakra*. It makes us conscious of our dharma or duty and gives us insight and understanding. If this *chakra* is not working well, it leads to deceit, dishonesty, chronic tiredness, inflexibility and a tendency to dominate. It could make one coarse, loud or insincere and even cause stuttering.

Chanting *mantra*s or any affirmations can help balance this *chakra*. Lie down under an open sky and try to absorb the azure hue of the sky. This has a positive impact on the *chakra*.

Colour: sky blue
Element: ether
Shape: A lotus with sixteen petals
Sense: hearing
Musical Note: PA
Sound: HAM
Aroma oil: sage and eucalyptus. Apply on the *chakra*.
Crystal: turquoise, aquamarine

Tarot correspondence: The Tarot Key number XVII: The Star. Focus your attention on the energies of the card and channel them to the *chakra*.

The sixth *chakra*: The *Agya* or the third eye *chakra* is the seat of wisdom and our higher mental powers. It is connected with psychic abilities, including clairvoyance and clairaudience. This *chakra* is also related to an understanding of existence, spirituality and hidden arcane knowledge. It is linked to our intuition, inner awareness and to our central nervous system. Saints or people who are spiritually evolved have this *chakra* fully opened.

A balanced Agya *chakra* gives us courage to do what we want. It gives moral courage, the sixth sense and the ability to face the world and stand by what you believe in. At a physical level, the imbalance of the *chakra* can cause sinus problems and headaches. It can also cause panic attacks, depression, arrogance and forgetfulness. At a psychical level, it can cause spiritual blindness, narrow-mindedness and lack of understanding as well as hinder the expansion of the mind.

To balance this *chakra*, lie flat on the floor and imagine an indigo light streaming in. Contemplate a deep blue starry sky. Close your eyes and imagine the expansion of the *chakra*. Sit before a lit candle and focus its light on the Agya *chakra*. Breathing exercises, pranayam or controlled, deep breathing and meditation help to connect with the energies of this *chakra*.

Colour: indigo blue
Element: none
Shape: a lotus with ninety-six petals
Senses: all senses, including extrasensory perception
Musical Note: DHA
Sound: KSHAM
Aroma oil: jasmine and mint. Apply on the *chakra*.
Crystal: lapis lazuli, indigo blue sapphire

Tarot correspondence: The Tarot Key number II: The High Priestess.
Focus your attention on the card of The High Priestess and channellize that energy to the *chakra*.

The seventh *chakra*: The Sahasrar or the crown *chakra* is located directly above the head. This *chakra* connects with the cerebrum cortex and cerebellum of the brain, the central nervous system, glands and hormones.

Activating and balancing this *chakra* is the aim of every spiritual seeker. It gives seekers awareness and enables them to let go of all egocentric activities, to trust the higher, divine guidance completely and to walk in the path of light. It is here that you merge with the divine and the separation ends. When you connect with this *chakra* you will experience pressure or a tug at the top of your head.

Ecstasy, bliss, thoughtlessness, self-knowledge, understanding and a spiritual connection with God are all characteristics of this energy centre. The Sahasrar *chakra* relates to full awareness of the self and of others. When this energy centre is fully developed, a seeker attains the level of a master. This *chakra* affects all other *chakra*s. Meditation will help to connect with this *chakra* and to connect with the inner being to develop fully conscious awareness. Time spent on mountain peaks, far away from earthly woes, helps in opening this *chakra*.

Colour: purple/white
Shape: A lotus with 1,000 petals
Senses: beyond senses
Musical Note: NE
Sound: AUM
Aroma oil: lotus, gotu kola (a herb). Apply on the *chakra*.
Crystal: amethyst, alexandrite, purple fluorite

Tarot correspondence: Tarot Key number XXI: The World. The energy of liberation in this card is supportive of this *chakra*.

Kabbalah and Tarot

'Kabbalah' is Hebrew for 'that which is received' and refers to a secret oral tradition of teaching, which extends from teacher to pupil. The word Kabbalah is applied to all Jewish mystical practices. The Kabbalist seeks a union with God through the exploration of mystical practices of Judaism.

Both Kabbalah and alchemy are based on the premise that through scientific methods, the consciousness can be awakened and doors opened to the esoteric knowledge that can empower mankind by realizing godhood in this life.

In both Kabbalah and gnosticism there is the belief that the soul that has descended from God is entrapped in the human body and the material world. The analogy is from an onion—like the layers of an onion, material concerns need to be peeled away to discover our true spiritual identity at the core.

A legend tells us that God taught the Kabbalah to some angels, who in turn, after the fall, taught it to Adam. The knowledge of Kabbalah was to help mankind return to God. It is thought that the biblical characters David and Solomon were Kabbalistic adepts. In Kabbalah, it is believed that each idea has its contradiction inherent in itself. This is also close to Hindu thought or the Chinese philosophy of yin and yang, which means that every good has a corresponding evil that needs to be understood and accepted.

The origin of Kabbalah has been traced to a book titled *Sefer Yetzirah* (Book of Creation), which was created in the tenth century. The central idea is that the created world is the reflected light of God. God created ten aspects or stations in life which we all have to cross and experience. These are the 'sephiroth'. There are twenty-two secret pathways that lead us to these ten aspects or destinations. All these concepts are visually represented in the Tree of Life, which is the central image of Kabbalistic meditation. Each of the ten stations is represented by a number in the range of 1–10. These correspond to the 1–10 numbers of the Minor Arcana cards of Tarot. Each sephiroth describes a certain aspect of God. The Tree also represents the path by which the divine spirit descended into the material world, and the path mankind must take to ascend to God.

Each sephiroth is a stage of development in our ascent to God. They contain the sacred name of God, representing the four worlds that the soul needs to understand and transcend. YHVH (the four Hebrew letters—Yod, He, Waw and He—that transliterate to Yahweh or God) is the Tetragrammaton (the name of the God of Israel as described by the Hebrew Bible) that needs to be understood by the spiritual seeker.

There are negative and positive forces at each stage that help and hinder a seeker. All esoteric practices help in fighting the negative forces and making quicker progress on the Tree of Life. Alchemy and Kabbalah have complicated texts, drawings, instructions that can help an adept. Among the plethora of esoteric instruments are the Tarot cards, which are also used in the quest. Just as there are twenty-two cards in the Major Arcana, there are twenty-two letters in the Hebrew alphabet and twenty-two pathways to the Tree of Life which leads to God, showing some correspondence among all these. An adept seeking to reach God must go through the experiences of the twenty-two cards or twenty-two pathways. Some practitioners even believe that Tarot is the pictorial representation of the Kabbalah.

The Fool's Journey. The Fool is the soul that has just come into being. He needs to go through various physical experiences to regain the divine consciousness. At every stage of his journey, he learns valuable lessons which help him to move ahead. These lessons are the twenty-two pathways of the Kabbalah, that finally reach Kether or the crown of the Tree of Life. In The Magician, he learns about the conscious use of the

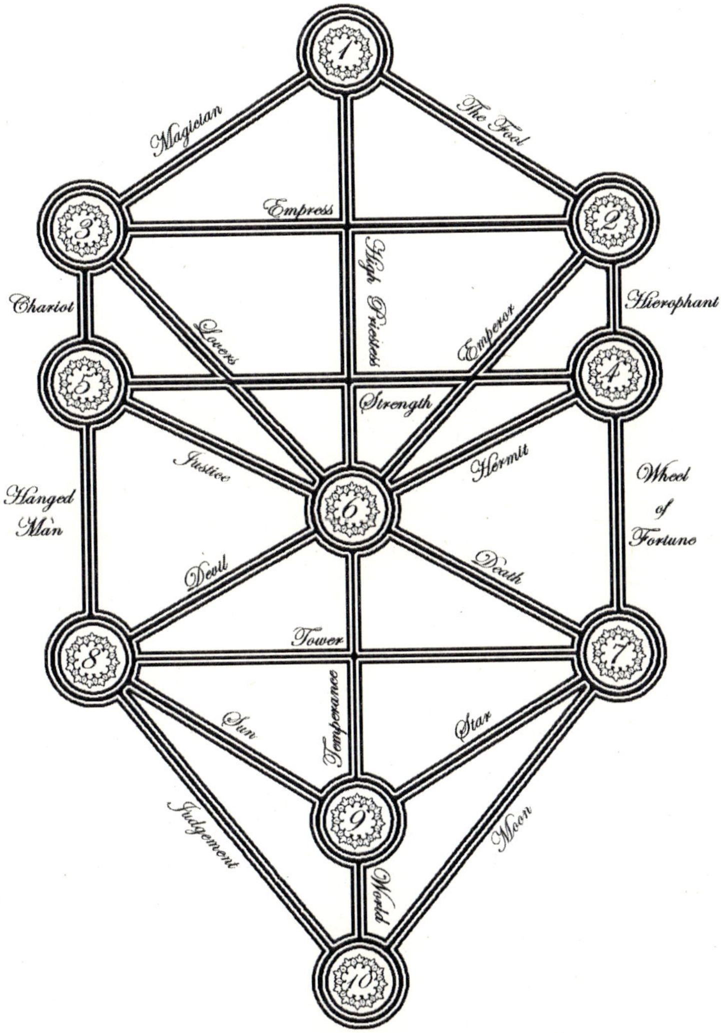

THE TREE OF LIFE

will and in the High Priestess he learns to connect with the unknown and the unconscious. In The Empress, he connects with the abundance that flows from the union of the conscious and the unconscious minds. In The Emperor and The Hierophant he learns about temporal power, social responsibility and the rules that need to exist in any society. In The Lovers he learns all about choice, harmony and human love. To be a Charioteer, he needs to conquer himself for it is only then that he will succeed in winning others. The Charioteer's courage and fearlessness comes from his integrity and confidence. In the card of Strength, The Fool learns that spiritual strength and faith lead to love and understanding of the beast within us. The Hermit, with his wisdom and his lantern of truth, guides him on the spiritual path.

With The Wheel of Fortune, he arrives at a juncture where he needs to observe life objectively like the blue sphinx without getting involved. Life will be in a constant flux and throw challenges at him, which is why he needs to remain aware and calm in the midst of the turning wheel of time. Whatever goes up will come down and whatever is down will go up. The lesson to be learnt is that it is essential to accept both and flow with the current of time. Divine justice may be different from human justice. Justice also needs to be tempered with mercy for it is only then that it is true Justice.

In The Hanged Man, The Fool surrenders himself to God and realizes that suffering is just a perspective. In the Death card, he understands that only when today dies, tomorrow can be born. If there are no endings, there would be no beginnings. For the new to come, the old must give way. Death should be welcomed for it means a new opportunity and a new tomorrow. In Temperance, he is healed by the Archangel Michael who shows him how he can, with the right combinations and modifications of the aspects of life, find the right blend leading to balance and harmony. He can transform his life through alchemy and create an elixir for true happiness. The Devil, he learns, actually signifies his own fears and weaknesses and if he confronts the Devil within, the Devil will wilt. The shackles do not bind him; it is only his choice that makes him stay chained to the Devil. In The Tower, the lesson is that a false edifice built on false premises and a blind ego will bring him crashing down. After these tough lessons, he realizes the true beauty of life with the correct insight given by the maiden in the card of The Star. Hope and love are close at hand if he would just see it. He knows then that there is a divine blessing.

The last fear is in the card of The Moon, where primordial fears come up to haunt him, where imagination creates a bleak landscape. There can also be poetry and creativity in The Moon but he needs to choose wisely. On the other side is the glorious Sun, offering happiness and freedom from the walled garden of limitation, with no need for control. The whole universe is there to support him. There is nothing to hide or fear and he rides forth on a white stallion. In Judgement, he makes the clarion call to all humanity to wake to the power of spirituality and to know that ultimately all will be forgiven. The Fool reaches the end of his journey in the card of The World, which is the final liberation from all bondage. He is a dancer in the dance of creation. He is united with the divine.

I CHING

I Ching and Tarot

Consulted for the wisdom in its pages—whether to draw gems of philosophy, statecraft and science or tools for divination from it—for thousands of years, *I Ching* is considered one of the oldest books in the world, with Chinese philosophers Lao-tse and Confucius credited as the authors of the text.

I Ching is made up of sixty-four hexagrams or combinations of short and long lines. It is based on the idea of yin and yang, which in short means that the universe is made up of duality, opposites that come together in various combinations to create the reality of existence. This echoes Indian thought, which also talks of *prakruti* and *purush*, or negative and positive aspects, as two ends of the spectrum of creation.

Yang is heaven, active, positive, male, firm, strong, light.

Yin is earth, passive, negative, female, yielding, weak, dark.

The philosophy behind *I Ching* is the Confucian premise, which propounds that an individual should flow with the Tao or the will of the universe, but seek harmony by appropriate action. *I Ching* helps in finding out the right action that will shape the person to achieve harmony with the family and society. It helps in the growth of the individual and an understanding of the universe.

Like Tarot, the aim of *I Ching* is the understanding of eternal laws that govern human existence so as to improve the quality of existence and to enable a human being to flow in harmony with the divine will. It assists the evolution of the human mind and soul and helps in learning the lessons that one needs to learn to evolve in life.

According to *I Ching*, the universe is made up of five elements—metal, fire, earth, water and wood—which influence human life. Tarot has four elements in the Minor Arcana—water (Cups), earth (Pentacles), fire (Wands) and air (Swords), which also influence human temperament and life. *I Ching* was first used just as an oracle with yang or the unbroken line meaning 'yes' and yin or the broken line meaning 'no'. To get more shades of meaning and to develop the oracle further, another two lines were added. These eight combinations are the core hexagrams and are called the *I Ching* family with specific propensities.

The sixteen court cards of Tarot, which exhibit certain specific temperaments, echo the hexagram family in *I Ching*. The *I Ching* family has eight core hexagrams or trigrams comprising a father, a mother, three sons and three daughters, which represent different states or stages of existence. They also represent certain processes of nature that can be applied to our lives and indicate certain situations. The hexagrams are combinations of broken yin lines (feminine) and unbroken yang lines (masculine), which indicate the possible flow of events and time. In the total of sixty-four hexagrams, there are different combinations of yin and yang, various permutations that reveal the ebb and flow of the universe and all its movements and functions, which reveal the seeds of things to come. Each hexagram contains a combination of ideas that can be deduced and then applied to questions posed to the oracle. This helps in understanding and modifying our actions to flow with our Tao. In this way, *I Ching* is a book of wisdom, which tells us what to do in order to mend our situation and improve our future. It helps us to improve our judgement or assessment about ourselves and our situation, making us wiser as it teaches us to flow with the universe, not against it.

I Ching Family

The father represents aggression, strength and movement.

The mother represents surrender and devotion.

The first son represents the initiating of movement.

The second son represents dangerous movement.

The third son represents rest and completion after movement.

The first daughter represents gentleness and penetration in devotion.

The second daughter represents clarity and the aspect of generousity in devotion.

The third daughter represents the joyous and still aspects in devotion.

It was the combination of these eight trigrams that created the sixty-four hexagrams.

Different scholars have tried to relate the Major Arcana of Tarot with different hexagrams. Here is one combination:

Major Arcana cards		Hexagrams
0	The Fool	19
I	The Magician	24
II	The High Priestess	15
III	The Empress	14
IV	The Emperor	27
V	The Hierophant	53
VI	The Lovers	8
VII	The Chariot	42
VIII	Strength	17
IX	The Hermit	58
X	The Wheel of Fortune	11
XI	Justice	54
XII	The Hanged Man	20/15
XIII	Death	59
XIV	Temperance	35
XV	The Devil	36
XVI	The Tower	3
XVII	The Star	40
XVIII	The Moon	6/10
XIX	The Sun	46
XX	Judgement	50
XXI	The World	1

Chapter Five

Healing and Rituals

5.

Healing and Rituals

The real use of any esoteric science is not so much in its predictive aspects as in the healing aspects that can act as a soothing balm to ease life and solve the problems that cause so much pain and stress to human beings. It should help you to learn the lessons that you need for your growth and development. Healing changes the thought patterns that cause so much havoc in our lives. It helps us to understand the self and connect with the positive energies of the universe. It helps us get what we need to live better and saner lives. Healing traditions of Tarot also give you the ability to see life differently and to get in touch with the larger scheme of things. It is about knowing how to shift the shape of your thoughts, feelings and attitudes to get the most out of life.

Healing is about transforming your life by understanding your being and connecting to divine possibilities. It is about applying natural laws and principles to everyday situations to heal yourself and the ills of this planet—for everything is connected. You are the world and the world is you. You influence the world and the world influences you. Your happiness will make the world happier too. We are not isolated individuals. Every action has a ripple effect; it is like a stone that we throw in water. Positive actions create positive ripples and affect so many people that we don't even realize the reach we have. A plethora of positive actions can change the destiny of this planet and save mankind from destruction. We are all magicians and can transform our lives with magic.

Evolution is the aim of existence. We are all born with some issues that we need to resolve in this lifetime. It is surprising how the same issue will keep coming up at regular intervals, causing devastation and pain till the lesson is learned and that particular issue is resolved psychologically in your being. Healing enables you to learn the lessons of life more quickly and saving yourself a lot of heartache and pain.

How does it help to know the future if you are not able to do anything about it? One would rather not know about it and live happily during the little time that is left rather than die a thousand times anticipating the problem. The point I am trying to make is that knowing the future is not enough—healing yourself and improving your lot is what will help.

Though destiny is something that we are all born with and which is more or less fixed, we all have a free will that can be used to modify the course of destiny and bring relief from problems. If you exercise your free will and choose the right action based on right thinking, on knowing what is correct for you—what is needed and what will ease the situation—most problems will become easier to handle. The right thinking comes from the right understanding and by not allowing your conditioning to bog you down and make you see every incident of your life through the prism of your past experience. Healing is about cultivating the right understanding and knowledge. Tarot and other esoteric sciences can, through meditation and exercises, heal your past and remove the scars that distort your thinking. They can help you to see situations as they are, to know and take the right action. Tarot can make you understand the lessons that you need to learn and help you dissolve the blocks that prevent release. Tarot helps us find the path by telling us what natural laws and principles are at work and how to work with them.

Symbols of Tarot are symbols of the universal mind and connected to it. They activate the unconscious mind, which is the all-powerful centre of the infinite—the power of the subconscious can make anything happen. Tarot can help you connect with the inner energies to fulfil your dreams.

Integrating the cards can help you deepen your understanding of yourself, others and life. The various aspects of yourself that you keep hidden, and are consciously or unconsciously avoiding, are seen, experienced and understood. It helps in understanding others as well for we see these aspects reflected in others and learn how to deal with them. To see life reflected in the Tarot cards gives you a closer look at it and makes you see it objectively and dispassionately. Affirmations help integrate the concepts and the symbols of the specific card in your mind to make that card a part of your being, bringing you its healing energies.

Through meditation, rituals and healing processes using specific Tarot cards, we try to reach the subconscious mind through images and pictures. We try to create an impression and influence our unconscious mind with the images of the cards. The mind thinks in visualized pictures and it is easier for an image to reach the subconscious mind than words. In words there can be distortion, but not in pictures.

Rituals are pictorial representations of what we want, enhanced by prayers, concentration and meditation. We ask the subconscious mind to create the feeling and the imagery of the cards in our life in manifestations. We use appropriate Tarot cards that convey the appropriate ideas and enhance it with harmonious colours, candles, flowers, crystals and the representation of the four elements. Through rituals, we can broadcast a plea to the universe for healing and fulfillment.

The universe is trying to give you what you want all the time. It is we humans who create the blocks through our own negative thought and behaviour patterns. We give wrong signals to the universe. The pictorial images of Tarot create the right images in the subconscious and bring similar circumstances into manifestation. We can invoke the law of attraction, which responds to whatever is broadcast to the universe and is joined by energies that are of an equal frequency, resonance, or vibration.

In this chapter, we will look at the use of Tarot cards for healing problems in different ways, through integrating the energy of the cards, through meditation, and some healing rituals that can bring about a change in your life. For example, through the *Surya mandala*, we can declare what we need to the universe. We add the power of our mind, hopes and expectation to the mandala (circle) as we draw on the energy of the sun. By looking at the mandala constantly and regularly, we impress the image and what it stands for in our mind and invite prosperity into our lives by accessing the power of the subconscious mind.

Healing should be done only for yourself. You should never try to undertake a process of healing for anyone else without their express permission because it would be encroaching on their private space and forcing your choice on the person. It is not only disrespectful, it is unethical. However good your intentions are, everyone has free will and the right to choose what they want to do or not do and you should not take that right from them. This is important to ensure that there is no negative impact from the healing process.

Some people believe that it is not advisable to interfere with the karmic law, but to experience what you have to. This school does not give any importance to efforts, realization and action as a means of dissolving karma and influencing the universe. Nor does it give credit to the value of free will and right choices that can dilute and destroy past karma.

There are other schools that think differently. They believe that karmic lessons can be learnt in many different ways. By healing your circumstances, you not only acknowledge your karmic lessons but you also dissolve your karma through righteous action and understanding. You impact your conscious and subconscious mind—and learn your lessons subliminally. It is about evolving by making the right efforts and and by reducing suffering with healing processes. Any kind of prayer, penance, or chanting influences the mind by clearing negative impressions. This is what healing does, but the choice is completely yours, for you must feel connected to the process.

Tarot can be used in many ways to heal yourself. It helps you to build your intuition and makes you aware of the best way to take your life forward with an inner conviction. It aids spiritual development through creative visualization and meditation.

With Tarot divination, you can affirm what you feel intuitively. It also brings forth your creativity and a deep understanding and spiritual knowledge of natural laws. It makes you come to terms with limitations and increases your faith in the goodness of the universe.

Tarot can be used in conjunction with other esoteric tools and systems such as crystals, runes, *I Ching* and astrology. Like these systems, Tarot is a way of exploring energies and vibrations. All these instruments help to reveal the unconscious and energetic processes of the human psyche. They help us to go beyond our rational, linear way of thinking, guiding us to a larger picture of existence and connecting us to the universal energies that can change negative patterns of thought. It shows a universal connection in life and how there is an interdependence of all aspects, which if respected, can lead to a meaningful and happy existence.

Crystals

Crystals are sources of energy that can help enhance our power of communication with the universe. They are the purest form of rock formation that exude healing energy, acting as amplifiers that can communicate our intentions. In the lost civilization of Atlantis, which is said to have existed about 12,000 years ago, crystals were considered a powerful source of energy and used extensively. This idea has received a huge impetus by the work of Marcel Vogel, a Nobel Laureate who has made startling scientific discoveries about the atoms in crystals that rearrange themselves, constantly emitting energy.

Crystals are formed by the solidification of lava and other fiery gases in the interior of the earth. The cooling and hardening of this mass forms rocks called crystals. Crystals and gemstones have been used for centuries by human beings for various purposes—to heal, protect, empower and connect with the higher, divine source. They have been used to enhance esoteric knowledge and spiritual growth. The crystals help in meditation, in calming the mind and in developing intuition, clairvoyance and clairaudience. Their use has been described in ancient texts, such as Indian and Mayan treatises, and there are references to gemstone healing even in the Bible. Most ancient civilizations believed in the positive influences of crystals and used them as diagnostic tools. The Romans and the Greeks believed that crystals have healing powers. In India, crystals have been long considered sacred with magical powers.

Even science uses crystals for various purposes, such as to magnify energy. Ruby crystals are used in lasers for microscopic surgery, while quartz crystals are used in ultrasound devices, watches and as memory chips in computers because they vibrate at a fixed rate when they are electrically charged.

Crystals, like all matter, are made up of atoms, protons, electrons and neutrons. These units are pure energy. Nobel Laureate Marcel Vogel was one of the first scientists to discover that crystals have an atom structure that is joined together in perfect harmony as if the atoms were holding hands. These free-flowing atoms arrange themselves into a specific pattern when the crystal is at rest. Crystals are sensitive to touch and movement, which stimulates the atoms to start moving. Energy is produced when the crystal is touched or moved. The atoms try to rearrange themselves to their original pattern and this reaction creates a loop that gives the user a constant flow of energy. The pattern to which the atoms always rearrange themselves is in harmony with cosmic energy and the terminated peaks connect with an infinite source. The crystals are capable of receiving and reflecting light, which is the highest form of energy in the physical universe. Vogel also discovered that crystals affect the molecular structure of water. After keeping a crystal in water for twelve hours, the taste of water changed and the impurities reduced. A human body is 70 per cent water and is, therefore, affected by the healing vibration of crystals.

The constant flow of energy from a crystal heals the mind and opens it to the cosmic oneness. It is an aid to meditation and development of intuition. The specific colours and compositions of the crystals make them suitable for specific problems. Crystal healing is about re-balancing and re-energizing the energy fields of the user.

The Major Arcana cards of Tarot have corresponding crystals that can enhance the energy of the cards and healing through the cards. It helps one connect better with a specific card and dissolve the obstacles to a specific issue or a *chakra*.

We are all aware of our weaknesses and the problematic issues that appear repeatedly in our life situations. Meditating on prescribed cards with the right crystal can magnify the healing energies of the card for the user.

Below is a list of the corresponding crystals of the Major Arcana cards. If you are unable to find the right crystal, you could always use clear quartz as a substitute.

The Fool: agate, tourmaline
The Magician: clear quartz/Tiger's eye
The High Priestess: moonstone/pearl /lapis lazuli
The Empress: carnelian/emerald
The Emperor: ruby
The Hierophant: emerald/hematite
The Lovers: rosequartz/alexandrite
The Chariot: amber/charcedony
Strength: topaz/cetrine

The Hermit: jade/topaz
The Wheel of Fortune: sapphire/adventurine
Justice: bloodstone
The Hanged Man: aquamarine
Death: black tourmaline
Temperance: rosequartz/aquamarine
The Devil: obsidian/black onyx
The Tower: garnet
The Star: turquoise/aquamarine
The Moon: moonstone
The Sun: amber/golden topaz/cetrine
Judgement: fluorite/Falcon's eye/malachite/fire opal
The World: opal/lapis lazuli/amethyst

Some Tips

1. Buying Crystals

When buying a crystal, go by what your heart tells you. Pick up a crystal that you are attracted to, but ensure that you don't buy a glass piece by mistake. Genuine crystals have natural inclusions or internal features.

To ensure that the crystal is not damaged or cracked, look at it against the light and so that you can see its core. If you are in doubt, you could consult experts or ask institutes that deal with crystals to check them out, but that could prove expensive. My advice would be to spend a lot of time in choosing your crystal and try to feel your way through. Trust your instinct and usually you will not go wrong. Himalayan crystals are considered best for healing purposes.

2. Purifying, Energizing and Programming

Every crystal needs to be cleansed, energized and programmed for it to be effective.

Purification Once you buy a crystal, it is important that you purify it. There are several ways to do this, but here is a simple method.

Take a small tub of water with enough water to submerge the crystal completely. Add a fistful of natural, unrefined sea-salt to it. Keep the crystal in this water, preferably outdoors, for twenty-four hours, then wash it with plain water.

Energizing Keep the crystal out in the sun to energize it for another twenty-four hours. The next stage is to programme the crystal.

Programming Before using a crystal for any purpose, one needs to programme it by affirming the specific purpose. Hold the crystal in your left hand, cover it with your right hand and repeat what you want the crystal to do for you three times. For example, if you intend to use it for the love ritual, programme it by saying, '*The powers of the universe, please clean these crystals of all negative and diseased energies, psychic programming and impressions. I invoke the healing powers of the universe to enter these crystals and help me find the perfect love of my life.*'

After using the crystals for a purpose, they need to be cleansed, energized and programmed before they can be used again. Please do not allow anyone else to handle your crystals as another person's touch would have a different energy from yours that will dilute or corrupt the programming. Should someone touch your crystals by accident, the process of cleansing, energizing and programming needs to be done again for the crystal to work.

3. Crystals for Specific Purposes

Crystals can be used in your home to create positive energy. The crystals need to be cleaned, energized and re-programmed every month to get the best results.

For positive energy in your home, use a lot of clear quartz chunks and clusters. Use five to six clusters with good peaks (unbroken and high ends) and scatter them in areas that you use the most, such as the kitchen, bedrooms, dining area and the family room.

For the energy of love, use large chunks of rose quartz and wear rose quartz pendants hanging where the heart *chakra* is, in the middle of your chest.

For mental clarity, use big amethyst chunks near the head of your bed.

To remove negativity from the environment, where there are too many electronic gadgets, use black tourmaline chunks in large numbers.

Clear quartz crystal is an all-purpose crystal that can be used to substitute almost any crystals.

Treat your crystal as something precious and valuable that has come to you to bring positive energy in your life and it will work wonders.

You could also put crystals in the floor or in the walls while doing up your home. Just take care that you don't damage the crystals or you could lose all the advantages.

Integration of the Cards

The images of Tarot are pictures of figures, symbols and landscapes that connect with the subconscious mind. Focusing on the card and integrating it into your being can help you understand aspects of the self and bring a new perspective on your circumstances and relationships. It will also help heal your mind.

Integration of the Tarot cards means connecting with them and allowing the energies of the card to reach you and have an impact on you. This connection is important to understand the cards and the energies that the cards hold. As the cards of the Major Arcana are aspects of the self, integration helps you understand yourself and others better. Once you are able to integrate the cards, you will notice the expansion of your understanding and sudden flashes of self-knowledge. You will recognize the specific energy operating in a situation or in a person, and with your understanding, will be able to manage them to an advantage.

There are various ways of integrating the cards. It is not an overnight process and requires time. It is like getting to know a person. Slowly, over a period of years, you build information about a person, like pieces of a jigsaw puzzle, and with time the picture becomes more detailed. The methods may seem very simple and childish but they do make a difference. Some practical ways of working with the cards are given below. These can be used with excellent results in combination with the mini-rituals described later.

1. If you are artistic, create a painting of the card and colour it with appropriate colours. This will help you to remember the card and the colours. You will connect to it much more and understand the significance of each colour.
2. Keep the right card in your purse and keep looking at it throughout the day. This will help build a closer connection and unconsciously, you will absorb the energies of the cards.
3. Keep the card under your pillow and allow it to sink into your mind subliminally.
4. Use the main colour of the card in your life. For example, if you are working with The Sun card, use a lot of yellows. The colour is a reminder of the image of the card.

5. Use all the five senses to connect with the card. If you can find the right herb associated with the card, make a light tea with it, slowly sip it and enjoy the feeling that the infusion creates. If there is an aroma oil associated with a card, apply it and experience the card through the smell. However, if you are not able to connect with these experiences, do not get anxious. Some people connect with an experience based on the senses, but others do not.
6. Assume the posture of the character and see if you connect with it in some way. See, for example, how it feels to sit like an emperor on a straight-backed chair, feel his sense of power and responsibility, his fearlessness and courage, his domination and leadership qualities. Try it—this will help you to understand his energy. Feel the pull of the energy and experience its flow.
7. Let the card become a companion and a friend and let it reveal inner messages to you. Let the card fill your mind space so that you can explore the card from different perspectives.
8. Keep the card propped up in your room where you can look at it constantly.
9. At night, just before going to sleep, look at the cards carefully and repeat the prayers given in this book.
10. Set the card up as a screensaver to constantly connect with it.
11. Write down what you like and do not like about the card. Add to your notes every now and then to build a detailed impression.

Mini-Rituals for Integrating the Cards

The best way to integrate the cards into your being is to work with each card of the Major Arcana for a week.

Connect to the card using the integrating methods described before in the daytime—one or more or all can help.

In the night, follow the ten-minute integration exercise given below with one card for seven days.

This mini-ritual can also be used to enhance and empower your daily meditation.

Before you start the process, it is important to prepare yourself by clearing all negativity. This could be done through a foot soak.

Foot Soak

1. Fill a tub with tap water, enough to cover your feet till the ankles.
2. Add a fistful of unrefined natural sea salt (not table salt). This salt is available at most shops.
3. Soak your feet for ten minutes in this solution. Keep a tumbler of water near you.
4. Remove your feet after washing away the residue with fresh water.
5. Throw the negative water in the toilet, not in a sink.
6. Ensure that the negative water does not spill anywhere, so be careful when you are rinsing your feet.

1. Key number 0: The Fool

What you need

Pale yellow silk altar cloth
One yellow and one white candle
Either carnelian or a clear quartz cluster
The Fool card
Incense stick
A small bowl of water
Yellow flowers

Process

1. Sit peacefully with the card of The Fool. Set up an altar in a place that is neat and clean. Spread the silk cloth.
2. Place the candles on your right and left and place the crystal and the card in the middle. Prop the card against a stand so that it can stay upright.
3. Light the candles and the incense stick in a holder. Place a small bowl of water in front of the card and place the flowers in front of it. Now your altar is complete.

4. Look at the altar intently for some time.
5. Take the card and hold it against your Agya *chakra* for some time to subliminally absorb the energies. The Agya or third eye *chakra* is located between the eyebrows.
6. Hold the card in your hand and look at the card, concentrating on it. Absorb the energies and the details of the card. Keep looking at it for some time. You could repeat the prayer to the Fool given in the second chapter slowly and deliberately.
7. Put the card back on the stand and keep absorbing the colours, candlelight, flowers, crystal and the impact of all these elements combined.
8. Repeat the affirmation for The Fool, slowly and deliberately, eleven times.
9. Close your eyes and recreate the image of the card in your mind's eye. Stay with it
10. After some time, blow off the the candles. Drink the water

Repeat this process with the card of the Fool for the next seven days.

Affirmations for The Fool

1. *I tread the path of life with joy in my heart and a smile on my lips.*
2. *Infinite possibilities are open to me for I trust life and welcome all experiences.*
3. *Life is full of joy if you have faith, hope and surrender.*

Do this process for each of the Major Arcana cards with the variations given below. The affirmation will vary with each card but repeat the affirmation eleven times for all cards. Choose any one affirmation from the options given that you connect with.

2. Key number I: The Magician

What you need

A white or red silk altar cloth
Two thick white or red candles
Red roses and white lilies or any white or red flowers—arrange them creatively

Representations of the four suits of Tarot cards and the elements they represent: silver coins for Pentacles or earth element, a bowl of water for Cups or water element, an incense stick in a holder for Swords or air element, candles for Wands or the fire element

A clear quartz crystal cluster

Process

Place the card of The Magician between the two candles against a stand. Surround it with the representations from the four suits of Tarot. Follow the integration process described above (Nos. 1–10), repeating the affirmations for The Magician eleven times.

Affirmations

1. *I can make anything happen in my life that I choose to.*
2. *I draw the power from above and manifest the will of God.*
3. *I can achieve anything that I want to. I have all the necessary prerequisites.*

3. Key number II: The High Priestess

What you need

A dark blue silk altar cloth

Two pillar candles, one white and one black, placed on either side of the card

A small mirror

A small scroll of parchment-like paper

A clear quartz cluster

White or blue flowers

A bowl of water

Incense stick and holder

Process

Prop up The High Priestess card on a stand between the pillar candles on the altar cloth. Place all the items in front of it. The parchment can be on the side.

Light the incense and candles. Look into the mirror and imagine the High Priestess's face superimposed on yours.

Follow the integration process, repeating affirmations for The High Priestess eleven times.

Affirmations

1. *I have all the knowledge that unveils in dreams and meditation. I am the secret knowledge that I seek.*
2. *I am the keeper of the flame of knowledge for eons.*
3. *I remind you of your inner eternity, the knowledge that will set you free.*

4. Key number III: The Empress

What you need

A green altar cloth
Two thick green candles
Red/orange flowers with green foliage
Crystal, a clear quartz cluster
A bowl of water
Incense stick and holder

Process

Place The Empress card between the two candles. Arrange all items aesthctically.

Follow the integration process with affirmations for The Empress eleven times.

Affirmations

1. *I am the mother goddess of plenty.*
2. *I nurture all creatures and make creativity flower.*
3. *Love and beauty flow through me eternally.*
4. *I am complete abundance.*

5. Key number IV: The Emperor

What you need

Red silk altar cloth
Two thick red candles
A bowl of water
Incense stick and holder
Crystal, a clear quartz cluster
A signet ring, crown, sceptre or any other symbol of power

Process

Follow the process with affirmations for The Emperor eleven times.

Affirmations

1. *I trust and depend upon my own power as others can trust and depend on me.*
2. *I have the discipline to achieve my highest ambitions.*
3. *I am The Emperor, the protector of all. Success and victory flow through me.*

6. Key number V: The Hierophant

What you need

A gold altar cloth
Two thick golden candles
Any kind of seal with wax
A bowl of water
Yellow flowers
Incense stick and holder
Crystal, a clear quartz cluster
Any small book of prayers

Process

Follow the process with affirmations for The Hierophant eleven times.

Affirmations

1. *I bring the known wisdom of the Universe to you to live peacefully with your fellow men.*
2. *Live successfully in this world with my knowledge of the past.*
3. *The tried and tested traditions bring respect within the society.*

7. Key number VI: The Lovers

What you need

Pink altar cloth
Four pink candles in four corners
Pink flowers arranged aesthetically

Crystal, four rose quartz pencils in four corners, pointing inwards
A bowl of water
Incense stick and holder

Process

Follow the process with affirmations for The Lovers eleven times.

Affirmations

1. *I choose freedom and harmony in all my relationships.*
2. *I choose to live my life filled with love, beauty and harmony.*
3. *Harmony within creates harmony without.*

8. Key number VII: The Chariot

What you need

White silk altar cloth
Two thick yellow candles
A bowl of water
Incense stick and holder
Crystal, a clear quartz cluster

Process

Follow the process with affirmations for the Chariot eleven times.

Affirmations

1. *I meet all challenges with confidence, joy and success.*
2. *I have won the toughest battle, which is with myself.*
3. *Victory is my nature. I live and breathe to win.*

9. Key number VIII: Strength

What you need

White silk altar cloth
Four yellow candles in four corners
Yellow roses arranged creatively
A bowl of water
Incense stick and holder
Crystal, a clear quartz cluster

Process

Follow the process and use affirmations for Strength eleven times.

Affirmations

1. *My perseverance and faith have triumphed over the beast within myself.*
2. *Love conquers all.*
3. *Strength is of the mind. It can conquer anything.*

10. Key number IX: The Hermit

What you need

A grey silk altar cloth
One thick, tall white candle
Four clear quartz crystals placed in four directions, pointing inwards
A rosary or a string of 108 telling beads
White flowers arranged creatively
A bowl of water
Incense stick and holder

Process

Follow the process and repeat affirmations for The Hermit eleven times.

Affirmations

1. *The path of enlightenment needs patience and inner illumination.*
2. *I follow the guidance of my inner being.*
3. *Wisdom is the light of the soul.*

11. Key number X: The Wheel of Fortune

What you need

White silk altar cloth

Four candles of different colours, yellow, green, blue and white, placed in four directions

Crystal, four clear quartz pencils placed in four directions, pointing inwards

Flowers of different colours

A bowl of water

Incense stick and holder

Process

Prop the card against a stand. Follow the process and use affirmations for The Wheel of Fortune eleven times.

Affirmations

1. *I am the blue sphinx, the observer of the tumult of time.*
2. *Luck will come with the turning of my wheel.*
3. *The centre of my wheel is stable—experience it.*
4. *Luck and good fortune attends me.*

12. Key number XI: Justice

What you need

White silk altar cloth

Four thick white candles in four corners; place the card of Justice against a stand in the middle

Red flowers and green foliage arranged creatively

Seal and wax or scales or a sword

Crystal, blood stone or a clear quartz cluster

A bowl of water

Incense stick and holder

Process

Follow the process with affirmations for the Justice card eleven times.

Affirmations

1. *Seek mercy with justice for who can face justice without it?*
2. *I seek balance in this turbulence and justice in all this injustice.*
3. *Divine justice always operates, but differently.*

13. Key number XII: The Hanged Man

What you need

Blue silk altar cloth

Two blue candles

Clear quartz crystal cluster

A bowl of water

Incense stick and holder

Process

Follow the process with affirmations for the card of The Hanged Man eleven times.

Affirmations

1. *I surrender to the higher purpose. God knows best and will take care of me.*
2. *I trust the divine, even in the suspended position, to take care of me.*
3. *I am powerful in my surrender.*

14. Key number XIII: Death

What you need

Black altar cloth
Two black candles
Crystal, a black tourmaline
A bowl of water
Incense stick and holder

Process

Follow the process with affirmations for the Death card eleven times.

Affirmations

1. *Without death, there cannot be life again.*
2. *I transform and renew myself and let go of the old and decayed to welcome the new.*
3. *Change brings a welcome relief.*

(Important: Not to be used except in special conditions under expert guidance)

15. Key number XIV: Temperance

What you need

Blue altar cloth
One blue and one gold candle
Crystal, kunzite or clear quartz cluster
White or blue or golden flowers

A bowl of water or a small chalice
Incense stick and holder

Process

Follow the process with affirmations for the Temperance card eleven times.

Affirmations

1. *My balance will bring harmony and healing into life.*
2. *I seek to transform base metal into gold and turn pain to pleasure, suffering to happiness and despondency to joy.*
3. *The elixir of life is the right combination of all aspects.*

16. Key number XV: The Devil

What you need

No altar cloth
Red and black candles
Crystal, one black onyx
A bowl of water
Incense stick and holder

Process

Follow the process with affirmations for The Devil card eleven times.

Affirmations

1. *From darkness and chaos, rise and find your light.*
2. *Confront me and gain ascendancy.*
3. *Face your devils and they will wilt.*

(Important: Not to be used except in special conditions under expert guidance)

17. Key number XVI: The Tower

What you need

No altar cloth
One red and one black candle
Crystal, one chrysocolle or a clear quartz cluster

A bowl of water
Incense stick and holder

Process

Follow the process with affirmations for The Tower card eleven times.

Affirmations

1. *I break down the old structures to liberate weakness and build afresh on the firm ground of truth.*
2. *The ego has to go to allow love to come in, sometimes causing pain.*
3. *Break the tower of the ego and become free.*

(Important: Not to be used except in special conditions under expert guidance)

18. Key number XVII: The Star

What you need

Light blue altar cloth
Three blue candles, placed in the form of a triangle, pointing down
Blue or golden flowers
Eight pointed tinsel stars; place them on the cloth
Some golden tinsel to sprinkle on the altar
A bowl of water
Incense stick and holder
Crystal, clear quartz cluster or turquoise or amethyst cluster

Process

Set up the altar, place the stars, sprinkle the golden tinsel all over and follow the process with affirmations for The Star card eleven times.

Affirmations

1. *I am insight and love, hope and care, after the dark night of the soul.*
2. *My stars shine, I bring healing and peace.*
3. *There is always hope and always joy.*

19. Key number XVIII: The Moon

What you need

Dark blue or silver altar cloth
Two dark blue candles
A silver coin
One moonstone or clear quartz cluster
A bowl of water
Incense stick and holder

Process

Follow the process with affirmations for The Moon card eleven times.

Affirmations

1. *Look for me beyond the real for I am imagination.*
2. *I shine through the reflected light of the sun.*
3. *Look through the illusion and go beyond to the sun.*

20. Key number XIX: The Sun

What you need

Golden yellow altar silk
Three yellow candles
Crystal, golden topaz or clear quartz cluster
Gold coin or any gold jewellery
A bowl of water
Incense stick and holder

Process

Arrange the candles to form a triangle, pointing down.

Follow the process with affirmations for The Sun card eleven times.

Affirmations

1. *I create life and love, joy and abundance for I am the centre of the universe.*
2. *I am the giver of life, light and brightness—I bring the same to you.*
3. *When I appear, all darkness disappears.*

21. Key number XX: Judgement

What you need

Grey altar cloth
Two white candles
Crystal, fluorite or clear quartz cluster
A bowl of water
Incense stick and holder

Process

Follow the process with affirmations for the Judgement card eleven times.

Affirmations

1. *I awake to the call of my spirit and know right from wrong.*
2. *All is forgiven and all is gained in the kingdom of heaven.*
3. *Listen to the divine call and become united with the source.*

22. Key number XXI: The World

What you need

Violet altar cloth
Three violet candles
Crystal, clear quartz cluster or amethyst cluster
A bowl of water
Incense stick and holder

Process

Arrange the candles in a triangle with the point facing downwards.

Follow the process with affirmations for The World card eleven times.

Affirmations

1. *Liberation is at hand—let us celebrate the dance of existence.*
2. *I dance to the divine song, which has no beginning and no end.*
3. *Liberation is the essence of existence.*

For a specific problem, use the healing meditation exercise given below, using the relevant Tarot card and the appropriate crystals. For different problems, specific cards are used and different methods of meditation apply. Please ensure that you follow instructions carefully to get the full benefit.

Mandala for negativity

This mandala (*mandala* is a Sanskrit word meaning 'circle'; the circle represents the universe and is used as an aid to meditation and spiritual healing in Hinduism and Buddhism) helps to heal psychological problems and negative emotions like fear and anger.

It is easier to do this with the help of an assistant as you are a part of the mandala and sitting within it.

What you need

Twenty thick, tall white candles and one large black candle
A round or square white mat
Eight clusters of amethyst
A large bowl of natural sea salt
Incense sticks and holder
A dinner knife
A small bowl of water

Eight amethyst clusters. Clean and energize the crystals (refer to the section on crystals). Hold the crystals in your left hand, cover them with your right hand and repeat the following affirmation three times:

The powers of the universe—please clean these crystals of all negative and diseased energies, psychic programming and impressions. I invoke the healing powers of the universe to enter these crystals and let them help me in clearing my fear and anger and fill me with strong positive energy.

Use the following eight Tarot cards after they have been freshly seasoned. To season the cards, pass them over incense smoke one by one so that the cards are cleaned by the smoke. This is called smudging.

Four Aces: the Ace of Wands to bring the fire element into balance; The Ace of Cups to bring the water element into balance; the Ace of Swords to bring the air element into balance; and the Ace of Pentacles to bring the earth element into balance.

The card of The Sun to remove the darkness of negative emotions and bring positivity, Temperance to heal and bring balance, Strength to give courage and energy and The Hermit to bring wisdom and objectivity. Large-sized Tarot cards (available in special shops) are ideal for this process.

To create the mandala

Spread out the mat and sit on it.

Create three circles around the mat. Let there be some gap between each circle.

In the outermost circle, arrange the twenty candles.

In the second circle, arrange the eight clusters of amethysts.

In the inner circle, first arrange the four Aces in four corners and in between the corners, place the other four cards. This will create a circle of eight cards. Place the cards below each crystal cluster. All the cards must face inwards.

Place one large black candle in front of you, and put all your negativity into it.

With the salt, draw a thick circle connecting the candles. There should be no break in the circle.

Place the black candle, incense stick and the water bowl within the middle circle.

Place a dinner knife by your side.

Take three deep breaths and start the process.

Light the incense

Now light the candles from left to right, invoking the elements to come and help you clear your negativity. Invite the earth element to nurture you, the water element to wash and energize you, the air element to blow away all cobwebs and the fire element to burn down all negativity.

Be careful that you have enough space all around you and that you don't catch fire.

An assistant could support you in this process so that you can relax. Take the knife and run it over your body slowly as if peeling the negativity off your body. Start from the head and end at the toe. Do this several times till you cover the whole body, front and back. After every movement, shake the knife on the black candle as if burning negativity in the candle. You should feel lighter. Put down the knife. Relax.

MANDALA

Imagine the lights from the candle making a circle above your head, settling on you and clearing you of all your problems. Take your time. Do it slowly. Relax.

Next, imagine the healing energy from the crystals also rising and meeting in the middle in a ring and settling on you. Take your time. Do it slowly. Relax.

Visualize the clearing of your negativity and feel a new strength.

Invite the energies of the cards to fill you, the four Aces to balance the elements with you, The Sun to bring brightness, Strength to give determination and courage, Temperance to heal your wounds and bring you in the right balance and the card of The Hermit to show you the right way of wisdom and experience.

Stay with this image in your mind for some time. Experience the peace and relaxation.

Slowly blow out the candle right to left and drink the water. Thank all the energies and the elements.

The whole process should take about thirty to forty-five minutes.

Keep the mandala as it is and spend twenty minutes every day sitting within the circle and repeating the process.

On the seventh day, allow the candles to burn down and sit there till all the negativity is symbolically finished. You could restart the process with fresh candles again the next day. You could repeat the process up to three times at a stretch—for twenty-one days. After this period is over, you need to give it a break.

The Prosperity or Surya Mandala

This mandala should be created and looked at every day for twenty-one days. The best time to connect with the mandala is at night.

What you need

A piece of cardboard (about twelve inches in size) with either golden yellow paper stuck on it very neatly without any cracks or painted golden yellow.

Blue tacks

Two thick golden candles

Two cetrine crystals clusters or clear quartz clusters

Incense sticks and holder
A small water bowl

The following seasoned Tarot cards: The Ace of Pentacles, Ten of Pentacles, Nine of Pentacles and the Knight of Pentacles.

To create the mandala

Concentrate to create a large face of the Sun with the curly and straight rays as shown in the Rider–Waite Tarot deck. Ensure that you draw it as artistically and carefully as you can, using appropriate colours. If you are not confident about creating it, you could download a picture of The Sun card from the Internet and print it out enlarged to A3 size. You could stick this on to a piece of cardboard.

Stick blue tacks in four corners and put up the four Pentacle cards. Place this mandala against the wall, with the two golden candles on either side. In front of the mandala, place the two cetrine clusters.

Place the incense stick and the small bowl of water next to the clusters.

Darken the room at night, light the incense and the candles and watch the mandala in this light. Focus your attention on the Sun and feel its rays filling your being. Stay with it for some time.

Now focus your attention on the other cards and feel the energy of money coming into your life. Imagine the Knight of Pentacles bringing in sackfuls of money ... see him bringing the money into your home and giving it to you. Feel the pleasure and satisfaction of the Ace of Pentacles when you get the money. Feel the family happiness and the security of the Ten of Pentacles and Nine of Pentacles that money can bring. Stay with the feeling.

After a little while, when you feel satisfied, blow the candles out and drink the water. Go to sleep, luxuriating in the feeling of being rich and prosperous.

Do this exercise in the night before going to bed. Keep the mandala in place for twenty-one days. It should be kept and worked upon in your bedroom so that you are connected with it.

All mandalas should be treated with utmost respect for them to work.

1. Designate a clear space for them, without clutter or dirt.
2. No one else must touch your mandalas.

3. Keep them away from prying eyes and curious questions.
4. Have a saltwater bath every day before you work with the mandala. Add a couple of tablespoons of sea salt in the last few mugs of the water while having a bath. Pour this over yourself and wait for five minutes before pouring tap water over yourself .
5. When you finish your work with the mandala, remove the cards from the board and smoke them clean with incense (smudging) and put them back in the deck. Clean the crystals in saltwater (refer to the section on crystals). The other materials, like the cardboard and the residue of the candles, should be thrown into the sea or any waterbody.

Handling depression

What you need

A full deck of Tarot cards

A crystal ball. Clean and energize the crystal ball before use (refer to the section on crystals).

To programme the crystal, hold the crystal ball in your left hand, cover it with the right hand and repeat the following affirmation three times:

The powers of the universe, please cleanse this crystal of all negative and diseased energies, psychic programming and impressions. I invoke the healing powers of the universe to enter this crystal and let it help me clear my depression and fill me with strong positive energy.

Light a candle and some incense sticks at an altar.

Sit down peacefully in an undisturbed place and breathe deeply in rhythm with your eyes closed. Relax.

Now try to understand what is causing your depression. It is important to identify the feeling. Go through the cards and find the card that expresses your feelings. For example, if you feel emotionally hurt you might connect with the Three of Swords, or if you feel humiliated and defeated you might connect with the Five of Swords or if you feel anxious and unable to sleep, you might decide to choose the Nine of Swords. If you look carefully, you will find the right card.

Bring out the appropriate card and look at it carefully, fully experiencing the feeling you get. If tears come to your eyes, let them flow. Take your time with this.

Next, look at all the Major Arcana cards and find one card that you feel can heal your pain. For instance, you might want to choose the card of The Sun if you think that brightness will dispel your dark mood, or you might feel that the insight and understanding of The Star will heal you or you might feel that Temperance will bring soothing balm and balance to your life. Choose what you think is the antidote to your feeling of depression.

Once you have identified the card that you feel could address your problem, put away all other cards. Keep the card in front of you.

Take the crystal ball into your hand and look into it with deep concentration. See the crystal ball expanding till it is life-size and you can enter it. Step inside the crystal ball and feel instantly energized by it. Feel your spirits lift. Explore the landscape of this new dimension that is safe and soothing. Take your time as there is no hurry, find a comfortable place inside the crystal ball and sit down.

Look at the Major Arcana card that you have selected for your healing with concentration. Feel the healing energies of the card. Let a healing beam emerge from the card and cover you fully. Stay with it within the crystal, and feel protected and loved. Let the light rotate on the pain. You will feel the pain lift.

When you feel healed and the pain disappears, thank the crystal and the card and slowly step out of the crystal. Let the crystal ball shrink to its original size.

Do this regularly to get results.

Clearing your Chakras with Crystals and Tarot cards

This process is best done with a partner though it can be carried out alone as well.

What you need

A candle
Incense sticks
A bowl of water

Seven crystals for the seven *chakra*s and the seven Major Arcana cards, corresponding with each *chakra* (as recommended in the fourth chapter). If you can't find appropriate crystals for every *chakra*, you could substitute them with clear quartz clusters. Use crystals that are cleaned and energized (refer to the section on crystals).

To programme the crystals, hold them in your left hand and cover them with the right hand. Affirm three times:

The powers of the universe, please clean these crystals of all negative and diseased energies, psychic programming and impressions. I invoke the healing powers of the universe to enter these crystals and let them help me clear all the chakra*s and fill them with strong positive energy.*

Place the candle, incense sticks and bowl of water at an altar and light the candle and incense sticks. If you are doing this process by yourself, keep the stones and the cards arranged in order on one side, close to you. If you have a partner, let them place the stones for you while you lie back and focus on the *chakra*s and the Tarot energy.

Take out the seven appropriate cards for the *chakras*. For the Mooladhar *chakra*, take The Fool; for the Swadisthan *chakra*, The Empress; for the Manipur *chakra*, The Sun, for the Anahata *chakra*, Temperance; for the Vishuddhi *chakra*, The Star; for the Agya *chakra*, The High Priestess; and for the Sahasrar *chakra*, The World. Look at the seven cards for some time before you start to meditate. If you find it difficult to focus on the energy of any card at this point, look at the card. Then, put them down and continue with your meditation but keep them handy and look at them if you need to.

Begin by breathing to centre yourself within. Take long, deep breaths and feel your body relax. Centre yourself and start the meditation. This takes about three minutes.

Begin with the Mooladhar *chakra*. Place carnelian or agate in the fork of your legs, firmly against your body. This is the *chakra* of survival issues, of the collective subconsciousness. Focus on the energy of The Fool and let the energy rotate in the Mooladhar *chakra*. Feel his innocence fill the *chakra*. If you find it difficult to connect with the energy of The Fool, pick up the card of The Fool and look at it carefully. Put it face down and visualize the energy. Feel the *chakra* expanding and vibrating. Stay with it for five minutes.

Next, place the coral on the Swadisthan *chakra*, which is located two inches below the navel. This is the *chakra* of the pleasure of the senses. Focus on the card of The Empress and allow her abundance and creativity to fill this *chakra*. Feel the *chakra* expanding and vibrating. Let the energies of The Empress fill this *chakra* and rotate there. Stay with it for three minutes.

Next, place cetrine/golden topaz or amber on the Manipur *chakra*, which is located two inches above the navel. This is the *chakra* of your personal power and emotions. Focus on the card of The Sun. Allow its brightness and power to fill the *chakra* with the energy of The Sun. Feel the *chakra* expand and vibrate. Let the energy of The Sun rotate there. Stay with it for three minutes.

The fourth *chakra* is the Anahata *chakra*. Place an emerald or jade or rose quartz or ruby on the middle of the chest where the *chakra* is located. This is the seat of love and compassion. Focus on the card of Temperance and let her balance and compassion fill the *chakra*. Feel the *chakra* expand and vibrate. Let the energy of Temperance rotate there. Stay with it for three minutes.

The next *chakra* is the Vishuddhi *chakra*, located at the middle of the throat. Place turquoise or aquamarine there. This is the centre for communication, creativity and good judgment. Focus on the card of The Star and feel the soothing energies enter it. Expand the *chakra* and let the energies rotate in the *chakra*. Stay with it for three minutes.

The sixth *chakra* is the Agya *chakra*, the seat of wisdom and occult knowledge. Place lapis lazuli or indigo blue sapphire in the middle of your forehead between your eyebrows. Focus on the card of The High Priestess and allow her secret knowledge to flow into the *chakra*. Let her lunar energies fill the *chakra*. Expand the *chakra* and allow the energies to rotate there. Stay with it for three minutes.

The last *chakra* is Sahasrar, the *chakra* of liberation. Place an amethyst on the floor and touch the middle of your head with it. Feel the vibrations. Expand the *chakra* and allow it to experience release. Take the leap and free yourself of all constraints. Focus on the energy of The World in this *chakra* and experience the true freedom of surrender.

Let all the *chakra*s rotate and experience the energy spiralling upwards. Enjoy the experience as long as you like. The experience usually lasts about forty-five minutes but it can be longer, depending on individual growth processes.

Gently remove the crystals.

After use, crystals need to be cleaned with natural salt water.

Ritual for attracting love and marriage

The rituals of Tarot constitute a formalized prayer to the universe to create circumstances in your life that are symbolically represented in the ritual. The ritual for attracting love and marriage should be performed with the purest intentions and total faith in the goodness of the universe.

You should never do the ritual for anything which is immoral and against the natural laws of the universe. Write down what you want to ask and repeat it exactly the same way every time you do the ritual. The right time to carry out the cycle is from the new moon to the full moon and should be done continuously. You can repeat the cycle. It can also be done for twenty-one days without a break.

What you need

A wooden table

Thirteen pink candles with stands

One new pink satin cloth to cover the table

A pink robe/pink clothes

Pink flowers

Incense sticks and holder

A small pink bowl with water in it—it should not be of plastic, but any natural material is fine.

Symbols of love or marriage (depending on what you want), such as a gold ring, green glass bangles, a *mangalsutra* or *sindhur*.

A quartz crystal cluster, thirteen crystal pencils (rose quartz pencils can be used instead of clear crystal pencils).

The following Tarot cards after being seasoned: The Lovers, The Sun, Temperance, The Wheel of Fortune, The Star, Two of Cups, Three of Cups, Ten of Cups, Four of Wands, Judgement, The Empress, Ace of Cups and Nine of Cups.

Use the Hierophant only if you are seeking marriage.

A passport photograph of yourself and your lover, if you have a definite person in mind.

Natural sea-salt to mix with water when you have a bath.

LOVE AND MARRIAGE RITUAL

Preparation

Collect all the items in advance.

Bathe, adding two tablespoons of sea-salt to the last few mugs of water. Rinse with plain water.

Wear pink clothes or a pink robe.

Prepare the crystals by cleaning, energizing and programming (refer to the section on crystals).

To programme the crystals, hold them in your left hand, cover them with your right hand and say the following lines three times:

Powers of the universe, please clean these crystals of all negative and diseased energies, all psychic programming and impressions. I invoke the healing powers of the universe to enter these crystals and bring true love to me (or bring a happy marriage) to me.

Lay down the pink cloth. Arrange the thirteen candles in a big circle. Connect the candles with flowers. Place each of the thirteen crystals below each candle. Place the incense on the top, outside the sacred space. Arrange the symbols of love or marriage around a bowl of water.

Process

Light the incense.

Invite the elements one by one to help you in the process. First invite the earth energies with crystals and flowers; water energies with the bowl of water; air energies with the incense; and the fire energies by lighting the candles.

Light the candles, from the left to the right, peacefully and with devotion.

Place your photograph in the middle of the sacred space. Place the card of The Lovers next to your photograph and imagine true love and the perfect soulmate entering your life. If you are using the photograph of your lover, place it on the other side of the card of The Lovers. Look at both the photographs and the card of The Lovers in the middle. Feel your lover's presence in your life like a sweet perfume that fills your soul. Feel your soul call out to your soulmate. Feel him or her coming into your life. Place the card of The Star above and feel the deep love that is given and received. Feel the insight and understanding that a true relationship has and brings.

Next, place The Sun card and the Temperance card on either side of The Star card and feel the intensity of your love, along with a perfect balance. Ask for a love that will drive all darkness from your life and leave you in harmony with the universe.

Next, place The Wheel of Fortune and The Empress next to Temperance and The Sun and feel the generosity of love, its warmth and demonstration in your life. Experience the exchange of love. Let luck bring you the truest and the best love that is possible. Place the card of the Judgement and let discernment enter your life. Place the Ten of Cups and the Four of Wands opposite each other and experience the happy unity of wedded life with a family that is content. Experience lasting happiness rather than temporary joy. Add the Two of Cups and the Ace of Cups to the circle and feel the spirit fill your cup of joy and see it running over. Feel the harmony and the ability to see any negative experiences through. Place the Nine of Cups and see your dreams come true. Finally, place the Three of Cups and see the celebration of a true relationship that has healing and cementing qualities.

For marriage, place The Hierophant above the circle presiding over the relationship. This is a marriage card. Imagine a happy marriage presided over by The Hierophant. He is smiling and giving his blessing. See yourself getting married and see your dreams come true.

Be sure that the placement of each card is appropriate. All cards should be facing you, not reversed. Go through each emotion and experience it. Each card relates to a happy relationship and you need to experience these positive emotions while placing the cards.

Concentrate on the spread, look at the flowers, crystals, the burning candles, the colours and the cards.

Repeat the affirmation given below or any other prayer that you want to or can devise.

The universe is in harmony with my plea
And opens the passage of true love for me
My lover comes with this flame
Drawn to me in thy name.

Our love is passionate, our love is true
Our love is eternal and will remain always new.

I call my lover in your name
So I desire and so it will be

For now till eternity
Let true love come to me
So it is, and so it shall be.

Repeat this affirmation three times with feeling, concentration and complete faith.

Close your eyes and stay with the power that you have generated. Ask for what you want. When you feel complete, open your eyes, blow out the candles from right to left, and drink the water in the bowl.

A Final Word

This book is meant to give the reader an introduction to Tarot, a foretaste, an understanding that esoteric sciences are not just fairy tales meant for desperate housewives with nothing better to do.

If I have helped you to look at these sciences with new eyes and with a more open mind, then I believe that my work is done. If you have realized, as a consequence of reading this book, that there is a method in this madness then the purpose of writing this book is served.

There is much more that needs to be said and explained—like divination and the innumerable spreads in Tarot. I have not touched upon them for fear of complicating the book and causing some confusion. The Minor mentors or the Minor Arcana cards have also not been explained in detail quite deliberately because too much information could burden the novice and may complicate the initial understanding of Tarot. An elaboration of the use of Tarot in combination with other systems like the runes, *I Ching*, astrology and Kabbalah has been left out for the same reason.

My aim is not to convert you to Tarot, but to encourage you to explore new ways that might give you solutions to your problems—ways that will open up new dimensions, that might question a rational approach and might seem absurd to start with, but entice you enough to give it a shot. It is to motivate you to try unconventional ways and see if they can offer you any respite or relief.

Often, the solution to a problem is staring at you in the face but you do not see it until a spark, a flash of insight suddenly helps you to look at the situation afresh. The answer unfolds itself right before your eyes. It has happened to me many times and I am sure most of us have experienced this. Tarot could be that spark that makes you think afresh and arrive at the answer to your problem.

Life is about experiences and perspective, efforts and hope. One keeps trying to see things differently, to find solutions and relief from the onslaught of time. This approach may just give you a new perspective and new hope. I don't know whether it will—but it may be worth trying.

Life is not always easy and we have all struggled with circumstances that have broken our backs and crippled our souls—we have lost the flame that we started out with. To me, life is a myriad-coloured kaleidoscope, which can rearrange itself in a variety of ways with the same glass pieces, but makes a particular pattern at a particular time.

I am trying to discover why those glass pieces create that particular pattern. I want to understand that image, connect with it and enjoy it. If the image is not what I like, I want to explore possibilities of affecting or influencing it positively in some way. Tarot is to me one of the instruments that can help me explore this path.

Where to Find Your Tarot Deck

Given below are suggestions to help you find Tarot cards, crystals and candles. These addresses are not recommendations by the author. They are given as a response to many queries that have been put forth.

Please check competitive prices and follow your intuition when choosing a deck.

The shops and areas referred to here are all in Mumbai.

The cheapest place to buy crystals is at Colaba causeway. There are many wheel barrows that sell good crystals. You should be able to discern and pick the right one. You can bargain and if you are buying more than one then you get a better price. My students went in groups and bought the crystals at half the regular price.

For candles the back lanes of Crawford market has a good variety of candles. Candles are also available at Bombay stores and other new age shops but the prices vary.

Tarot cards are available in most bookshops like Crossword, Landmark, Oxford and others.

Specialized shops include

1. D Tarachand
   283 Janikar Street

Opposite Jumma Masjid
Crawford market
Mumbai 400002
Contact Anil Bijlani
Tel. 022 23427057
Mobile 09819913925

2. Energy Systems
   Jalaram nagar building
   Office no. 12,
   SVP Road
   Chamunda Circle
   Borivali
   West Mumbai 400092
   Contact Bhavesh A Vadia
   Tel. 02228903570
   Mobile 9820392420

3. Ostara New age shop
   Phone 022 23874929

Others places you may wish to explore

1. Om enterprise
   Liberty Gardens
   Malad West
   Mobile 9820722333

2. Tarot for all
   Gokhale Road
   Naupada W Thane
   Mobile 9321606522

3. Wiccan Alter
   Thakur Village
   Kandiville East
   Mobile 9930877962

For Crystals:

1. Mikao Reiki & Crystal Centre
   Chiku Wadi
   Borivilli West
   Mobile 9967549070

2. Crystal Rock Shop
   Laxmidhar
   195 Shreeram Building
   CR street
   Dobhi Talao
   Phone no 222078449/ 222078450

3. Amrita
   Mobile 9892214156

Good luck !